P9-DJV-649

THE BICYCLE

In Life Love War
and Literature

THE BICYCLE
in Life Love War and Literature

Seamus McGonagle

SOUTH BRUNSWICK
NEW YORK: A. S. BARNES & CO.

First American edition published 1969 by A. S. Barnes and Company, Inc., Cranbury, New Jersey 08512.

Library of Congress Catalogue Card Number: 70-81688

SBN 498 07450 1

Printed in the United States of America

To my father,
who remembered the words of
'Daisy Bell'

FOREWORD

In *The Times*, of London, on October 14, 1967, Mr John Osborne, the well-known playwright, reviewing a book on the theatre had this to say:

'Mr Russell Taylor's book takes us trippingly through the Landseer school of dramatists, from Scribe through Pinero to Rattigan, with the pleasing proposition that there is still a place for the well-made play. I wouldn't care to argue about this, much less to go to the excess of writing a book about it. There is a place for the bicycle and I wouldn't deny anyone a book on the subject . . .'

Read on, Mr Osborne.

SEAMUS McGONAGLE

PREFACE

The bicycle, like corsets and McGill seaside postcards, is a subversive survivor. Subversive because it uses the tricks of the good soldier Schweik to survive, bringing on its head a good deal of friendly but uneasy derision. It obeys the rules but somehow contrives to break them at the same time. It has a way of leaving a hint of conspiracy in its wake. People who ride bicycles are different! The bicycle itself is different, and was different at its birth.

A hybrid which developed in between the great inventions of the Industrial Revolution and the Twentieth Century, while managing almost completely to ignore both. A child of the great pause between the steam engine and the internal combustion engine. A real yeoman of a machine whose development seemed almost a retrograde step.

But there is no denying that it has penetrated the consciousness of writers as disparate as H. G. Wells and Samuel Beckett. Perhaps it gave these writers a loophole, in that they could use the bicycle as a link with a more serene age without actually being accused of ignoring an existing technology. This very esoteric use of the bicycle would no doubt raise a smile on its face, were it human; for right through its birth, adolescence and middle age, the bicycle has, Schweik-like, presented an attitude of extreme flexibility to human whims while maintaining a secret integrity. Survival, after all, is more important than posturing. It was first of all a plaything of the aristocracy, then a status symbol of the rich middle class, and eventually, in its boisterous coming-of-age, a symbol of the working class's right to inexpensive leisure pursuits.

The bicycle's survival factor has meant that it has changed shape from time to time—sometimes subtly, sometimes radically, sometimes with the hint of a devilish joke at human expense. The early 'hobby-horses' and 'boneshakers' gave way to the faster penny-farthings which were much more difficult to ride because of the size of the front wheels. These, in their turn, gave way to the safety models with chain drive and which looked exactly like the earlier hobby-horses with their equal-sized wheels.

One of the finest examples of this survival factor is the Moulton small-wheeled bicycle. Just at a time when everyone except the enthusiasts was saying 'The bicycle is finished', along came this mini-wheel bicycle to catch the imagination of everyone from small boys to leading figures in public life. Just when society is expecting the bike to retire into genteel but impoverished widowhood, there she goes donning a mini-skirt, flaunting it down the street, scandalising the more sedate neighbours and 'hallooing' down the valleys of the motor-car-conscious bourgeoisie. Good luck, merry widow!

S.MCG.

ACKNOWLEDGMENTS

That this book exists at all, is mainly due to the enthusiasm of Lesley Ann Vernon and the encouragement of Jock Webster, to both of whom I am eternally grateful.

I must also thank Mr Derek Roberts of the Southern Veteran-Cycle Club; Mr Philip Sumner of the Science Museum and the staff of that museum's library; the staff of the Imperial War Museum Library; Mr Malcolm Pleasants, and Mr Barry Knowles.

It is, of course, impossible to mention individually the numerous other people who helped in various ways, especially those who related anecdotes to me. I can only hope they think I have put their help to good use.

January, 1968

CONTENTS

ILLUSTRATIONS

Pictures number 2, 3, 4, 5, 6, 7, *reproduced by courtesy of The Science Museum; pictures number* 1, 9, 10, 11, 12, 13 *by courtesy of Radio Times Hulton Picture Library.*

1

'TRAVELLING WHILE SITTING DOWN'

There is a story of an African who, on seeing his first bicycle, mounted by an Englishman, exclaimed, 'Trust the English to invent a way of travelling while sitting down.' A humorous remark and fairly accurate about the English, it is not in the least accurate about the invention of the bicycle. In fact, the origins of the bicycle are almost as obscure as the origins of Gothic architecture, or at least as anonymous. Fathered by the remnant of a dying feudal system, mothered by the still young Industrial Revolution, the bicycle—with the horny-handed, ever present human curiosity and inventiveness as mid-wife—was born around about the tail end of the eighteenth century.

Any attempt to give an actual date is to court rebuff from that small band of eagle-eyed historians who delight in informing their less-informed fellows that, for instance, Napoleon chewed licorice after dinner and not mint, and that Finn McCool was actually seven foot two-and-a-half inches tall. There are, however, in the bicycle saga some key dates and names.

One of these dates is 1791 and one of the names mentioned is that of the Comte de Sivrac. The effect he had on the populace when he appeared in the gardens of the Palais-Royal astride a small wooden horse fitted with two wheels could probably be equalled today by someone astride a plank carried by two balloons, say, floating at shoulder level down Oxford Street. (Wouldn't a small floating jet-propelled craft be more dramatic? it might be asked. Ironically enough, probably not. People today are so blasé about the fact as well as the fiction of space travel, that it would take something really outlandish like your two balloons and a plank to raise an eyebrow.)

However, de Sivrac's bicycle on that historic day caused quite a clamour. After the initial surprise, it probably raised quite a laugh as well, for it was propelled by thrusting at the ground with the feet, first one and then the other. It had one big disadvantage. It could not be steered by turning the front wheel. So, except for small deviations from the straight line by banking the machine by leaning to the side, the rider could only proceed in a straight line. Nobody has recorded what de Sivrac did when faced with a tree or a house while he was travelling down a hill, or if he was ever actually foolish enough to point his machine in the direction of one of these obstacles.

It is worth noting that de Sivrac's machine was not called a bicycle at this point in its career but a *célerifère*. And it had probably existed as a child's toy for some time before. Toy it remained for some time after, but this time a toy of adult aristocracy. It was renamed the *vélocifère* in 1793 and became very popular as a new pastime with the *Incroyables* under the Directory in France. By all accounts, the gardens of the Palais-Royal were positively littered with the young men of the day, dressed in the height of Directory fashion riding these *vélocifères*. (An eighteenth-century parallel, perhaps, of the 'mods' of England in the mid-sixties of this century and their motor-scooters?) In fact, the new pastime became so popular that the riders—or velocipedes, as they were then called—combined into a sort of club and organised races along the Champs-Elysées.

Before going any further, it is interesting to ponder a mystery at this stage. Although de Sivrac is generally associated with the first bicycle as we know it, there is in a church in Stoke Poges a stained-glass window which was made in Italy around 1590. Nothing startling in that, except that the centre portion of the window shows a cherub sitting on a two-wheeled machine which looks amazingly like the de Sivrac bicycle! If the Italians did discover the bicycle, they kept very quiet about it, though it would not be surprising for at that time Italian artists and inventors were practically leading the field in new discoveries. In fact, Leonardo da Vinci was so busy designing various amazing machines at the time that it is just possible he stumbled on the idea of the bicycle. Incidentally, the Stoke Poges church mentioned is the one where Thomas Grey, the English poet, finished his famous *Elegy written in a country churchyard*.

As the eighteenth century gave way to the nineteenth, the gathering political storms most likely put paid to the flippant cavortings of the young Frenchmen and their odd playthings, for they were little heard of in the teens of the new century. That is, until a year after the Battle of Waterloo. For it was in 1816 that another Frenchman, Nicéphore Niepce, of Chalons, produced an improved *célerifère*. This one had a simple wooden horizontal beam with a carving of an animal's head on the front, mounted on large-spoked wheels. What made it different from the earlier machines was that it was lighter. This may not impress the modern reader so much, but it is equivalent to the Gothic stonemason's discovery that thinner columns of stone will still support a building, which eventually led to the beautiful flying buttresses of the fifteenth century. An indication of the range of these early bicycle innovators' activities can be gathered from the fact that Niepce is better known as the 'Father of Photography'. Mind you, the front wheel of his bicycle was still not steerable although some historians think that Niepce added this refinement at a later stage.

Niepce's machine was merely a curtain raiser for the really big name of this period—Charles, Baron von Drais, of Sauerbrun. Baron von Drais is best described as the Henry Ford of his day. He gave the bicycle the front steering wheel and, by popular assent, his name to the machine. Above all, he lifted it out of the world of fashion and novelty, giving it utility and purpose which it never had before.

Charles von Drais was chief forester for the Grand Duke of Baden, a job which suited his agricultural bent. But he was also an engineer. His forestry work took him over many miles of forest and rough land, a lot of which was steep and hilly. Prompted, no doubt, by the weariness of trudging over this tiring terrain, he evolved in the early part of 1817 an improved *vélocifère* which had a partially-triangulated wooden frame, a steerable front wheel, a padded saddle and an arm rest to hold on to when thumping the ground with the feet. Of course, the steerable front wheel was the real *coup de grâce*. How otherwise to negotiate the tortuous forest paths? The following year he had even more improvements, and finally the machine was exhibited to the public for the first time in April 1818, in the gardens of the Luxembourg. It was immediately dubbed the 'Draisienne', a fitting tribute to the Baron, who earlier that year had been granted a patent for his machine:

'We, by the grace of God, Grand Duke of Baden, Grand Duke of Zahringen, grant to Karl, Baron of Drais, for his invention of a tread machine, an invention patent for ten years' duration that no one can copy or have copies in the land of the Grand Duchy or shall use this on public streets or place, without having first gotten proof of it from him.

Granted January 12, 1818.'

It was also in this year that the bicycle got the name by which it was to be known for at least another fifty years. A patent taken out in Paris in late 1818 for a similar machine referred to it as a velocipede, and this name was generally used until about 1870 when the word 'bicycle' appeared in a Patent Office specification.

Baron von Drais had done a good job of public relations for the Draisienne. Most people today would accept as axiomatic that cycling was faster than walking, and would probably suspect the sanity of someone who argued otherwise. In 1818, people had to be convinced by practical demonstration, and this the Baron had done. Shortly after, the velocipede was adopted in England, Germany and the USA. Claudelle Niepce, brother of Nicéphore, was living in Hammersmith at the time, and had obviously been following the fortunes of his brother's machine as well as the Baron's with some interest. On December 21, 1818, he wrote to his brother in France, pointing out that a great deal of interest in the new machines had been shown in England. The *entrepreneurs* of the day must have worked really fast, for another letter from Claudelle to Nicéphore dated August 1819 states that the machines were in fact in England in great quantity, and were proving extremely popular.

The prime mover on the English scene was one Dennis Johnson, coachmaker, of Long Acre, London. He copied von Drais's design and renamed it the 'pedestrian curricle'. It became immediately popular with the Corinthians of the Regency and was called, among other things, the 'dandy-horse' or 'hobby-horse', the former name probably referring to the nickname of the period for the young Regency bucks.

A poem in an English magazine of the time gives a clue not only to its popularity but to one of the many names it was called:

Though some perhaps will me despise,
Others my charms will highly prize

Yet, nevertheless, think themselves wise.
Sometimes, 'tis true, I am a toy,
Contrived to please some active boy;
But I amuse each Jack O'Dandy,
E'en great men sometimes have me handy,
Who, when on me they get astride
Think that on Pegasus they ride.

The author of the poem remained, with more than an element of good sense, anonymous. But a finer poet, John Keats, referred to the velocipede in 1819 as 'the "nothing" of the day'. One of the leading magazines, *Ackerman's Repository of Arts and Sciences*, examined the von Drais machine in its February edition of 1819, under the headline:

'A CURIOUS INVENTION'

'The principle of this invention is taken from the art of skating, and consists in the simple idea of a seat upon two wheels propelled by the feet acting upon the ground. The riding seat or saddle, is fixed on a perch upon two double shod wheels running after each other, so that they can go upon the footways. To preserve the balance, a small board, covered and stuffed, is placed before, on which the arms are laid, and in front of which is a little guiding pole, which is held in the hand to direct the route.

'The swiftness with which a person well practised can travel is almost beyond belief—eight, nine and even ten miles may, it is asserted, be passed over within the hour on good level ground. The machine, it is conjectured, will answer well for messengers, and even for long journeys; it does not weigh more than fifty pounds, and may be made with travelling pockets. The price, we are informed, varies from eight to ten guineas.'

Hundreds of these machines were made and sold, and it was a common sight to see the young men padding along the streets and through the parks. It is not too wild a conjecture that, if George III had survived a few more years, he would have been driven to his demise by the latest craze of the young men of his realm. On the other hand, who knows, but that a wild sprint down the paths of the London parks on one of these dandy-horses would not have been wonderful therapy for the mad old king?

It is an interesting comment on the so-called satire of today that the caricaturists of Regency days were more vicious, daring, scurrilous and provocative than any since. With the new Regency craze they had a hey-dey. Cruikshank, Rowlandson, Leech and Alken all went to town on the hobby-horse—metaphorically speaking, that is.

Drawing after drawing poured from their fertile pens, ridiculing the new machine and the young men who rode them. In fact, so severe was the mockery it is almost certain that the caricaturists single-handed did the craze to death. So much so, that after 1822 to be seen riding a hobby-horse was to invite the derision of any passer-by. In this century, David Low was probably the only cartoonist whose work approached a comparable effectiveness. A cartoon by Cruikshank was captioned: 'A new Irish jaunting car by which you can ride at ease and are obliged to walk in the mud at the same time'. Another mocker of the time remarked of the hobby-horse: 'Some apprehension appears to have prevailed that the national breed of the genuine animal would suffer from this daring competition.' One particularly acid drawing shows the Prince Regent lying face downwards on a hobby-horse with a rather large buxom wench sitting on his back. But another drawing in 1819, though satirical in purpose, unknowingly anticipated the motor-cycle. The drawing, titled 'Velocipedraisiavaporianna', shows a steam engine mounted on a hobby-horse. It is thought that this drawing originated the idea of the motor-cycle, and one of these steam-driven monsters was actually built in 1868 or thereabouts.

In spite of the fact that velocipedes fell out of popular use after the early 1820's, they were still used and improved upon by the inventors, mechanics, mathematicians and enthusiasts of the day. In 1830, a Monsieur Dreuze, an official in the

French Post Office, persuaded the government to mount rural postmen on an improved Draisienne which he had brought out. During the summer of that year, all went well and the mail arrived a lot earlier than it had ever done before. Bad luck, however struck in the form of a snowy and miserable winter. The postmen's velocipedes became unmanageable on the icy roads, and the postmen suffered many a cracked head and rib. The experiment was called off.

Michael Faraday, the inventor and electrical genius, used to ride a velocipede around his workshop, and it is reported that in 1836 he astonished the residents of Hampstead by riding one around the village. It is quite probable that the residents of Hampstead would be equally astonished today to see one of these machines ridden through their streets.

It must be remembered that, at this stage in its career, the bicycle was still propelled by the feet on the ground. So far, no one had thought of fitting a crank to either one or other of the wheels.

And so the great 'velocipeding versus walking' debate continued. In a scientific journal of the 1830's, one enthusiast went so far as to prove that velocipeding was superior by using the laws of physics and mechanics:

'Walking requires a tractive force equal to 1/13th of the man's weight. A wheeled vehicle on a gravel road (one of the worst) requires 1/16ths of the gross weight; on a well-macadamized road about 1/40th; on the best London pavement 1/70th; on the well laid flagstone 1/80th; and on a railway 1/224th. If we take a man's expenditure of force in rowing or working a velocipede as equal to 53 ft./pounds per second, and 30 miles equal to a day's walking, we shall find that a man weighing 150 pounds on a velocipede weighing 80 pounds (and we should remember that the weight of the best machine does not exceed 56 pounds) will travel on a road where the traction is 1/40th from 50 to 60 miles easier than he will walk 30, even if he uses a four-wheeler. On the best London pavement he might travel 90 to 100 miles, and on a railroad about 270 miles a day.'

Which some people might consider an extreme case of using a steamroller to crack a nut. But the seriousness with which these problems were taken at the time is reflected in the following problem and answer published in the *Mechanics' Magazine* of 1831:

'How can a man, without touching the ground, or having any lever or instrument in his hand or elsewhere, wheel himself up the steepest road in the kingdom in a common wheelbarrow?'

The problem-setter comments at this stage that there is no trickery in this, and manages to keep a straight face when giving the answer:

'Let a man take a common wheelbarrow without addition of any kind, having an ordinary sized wheel of 18 or 20 inches in diameter, and (as very steep ground may not be near) let a square bar, of one inch thick, be put in front of the wheel, on hard level ground which will be equivalent to a hill rising more than one in three; then let him mount the barrow, and without his touching the ground, cause it to wheel with him in it, over the bar.

'A medium effect will be produced by sitting on the foreboard of the barrow with the wheel between the legs, and pushing the wheel round with the hands. But as the problem is a maximum, it can only be solved by standing astride on the side bars of the barrow, a little in advance of the axle, with the face towards the barrow, laying hold of the wheel by its felloes, and pulling, or rather throwing all the weight of the body backward, which will draw the wheel and all with it over the bar.'

The absurdity of sitting in a wheel barrow to prove the efficiency of velocipeding was not lost on this problem-setter's contemporaries. Writing a few years later, one of them dismissed the whole idea with due sarcasm:

'It is quite possible to sit in a wheelbarrow and to wheel yourself up a steep hill, but the position is so uncomfortable, and the process involves an infinitely larger expenditure of forces than walking, therefore we never see reasonable men exercising themselves in this way.'

Although the crank was not fitted to a wheel until later, a Lewis Gompertz of Surrey in 1820 made a device to supplement the leg action on the ground. This gadget was worked by the arms, the steering handle was provided with a toothed quadrant at the lower end, and this engaged with a pinion on the front wheel hub. When the handle was pulled backwards, the wheel turned, and a free-wheel device in the pinion allowed the handle a free return to its original position.

The Gompertz gadget is thought to be the first workable driving mechanism added to the hobby-horse, earlier attempts having failed due to over-complication. If some of the Gompertz principles had been refined and developed—especially the free-wheel pinion—the bicycle as we know it today would probably have arrived a lot earlier. But that is hindsight wisdom, and the bicycle took its own circuitous path of development.

It must not be thought that, even as early as the 1820's, velocipeding was exclusively a man's sport or pastime. In 1819 Dennis Johnson also made a ladies' hobby-horse. The cross-bar or frame was dropped low for obvious reasons, the front part following the curvature of the wheel, and the back part being horizontal and about six inches above the ground. The wheels were of wood, with iron tyres and the saddle was supported on a pillar of iron rising from the horizontal part of the frame. One big drawback was that it weighed 66 pounds, which is probably the reason it did not become popular!

As has been stated previously, the hobby-horse went out of fashion in the late 1820's, and was used only occasionally after that. Some of them survived for a considerable time, however, and one report tells of one which was ridden regularly to market by a Northamptonshire farmer well into the middle of the nineteenth century. One can just imagine him saying: 'By golly, I invested in this 'ere machine, and fashion or no fashion, I'll use it till it falls apart!'

Now the history of the bicycle, like the history of any other revolutionary machine, is punctuated by technical breakthroughs. Some are small and of only marginal significance, but some open up new chapters. It might be said that the contribution of the Scotsman, Kirkpatrick Macmillan, to the bicycle epoch not only opened up a new chapter, but started a new volume of the book whose first volume had ended with the 1820's. For Macmillan was the first person to discover and fully appreciate that a road machine with two wheels in line could be balanced, and at the same time, propelled forward by the rider, operating a system of treadles and cranks connected to the rear wheel hub. Macmillan was a blacksmith and engineer who lived in the village of Courthill in Dumfriesshire, and it was the practical repair work which he carried out on hobby-horses at his forge which gave him his brilliant new idea for propelling the machines. And all this in 1839, from which date Macmillan frequently rode his 'bicycle' the fourteen miles between Courthill and Dumfries. He once rode all the way from his home to Glasgow, a distance of forty miles. Even if Macmillan's position as a major figure in the story of the bicycle were not assured, which it most certainly is, he would at least be remembered for his contribution to minor cycling history. In 1842 he was fined five shillings at the Gorbals Police Court in Glasgow for knocking over a child with his bicycle. This was the first ever cycling offence to be officially recorded.

Although Macmillan's machine was copied to a certain extent during the next twenty years, it did not become very popular, in spite of the fact that it anticipated the rear-drive safety bicycle by some forty years. One of these copyists, Gavin Dalzell, a cooper of Lesmahagow, Lanarkshire, was for some time credited with the invention of the machine in 1845. But in 1892 the credit was, properly, given to Macmillan. Either way, it affords Scotsmen a harmless bit of chauvinism, in that Scotland at this time led the world in its contribution to the bicycle. Macmillan's machine also probably inspired the following wry piece of Scottish humour, which was recounted in a magazine of around 1850:

'In 1843, in Edinburgh one morning, the news had spread like wildfire that a shoemaker had, the previous day, outdistanced the Glasgow "Highflyer" coach with four greys in it! They say it took the shoemaker, on and off, thirty years to perfect his machine, which was a velocipede. Crowds of people flocked to the shoemaker's stall (his name was Crispin). Among them was a gentleman who was an enthusiast on velocipedes. He asked Crispin if it were true that he had passed the Glasgow coach on his machine.

'"Quite true," said Crispin. "But there's one thing ye should ken." "And what's that?", said the gentleman. 'Well sir," said Crispin, "it's jist this—I was gang wan way—and the coach was gang the ither!"'

From about 1845 the principle of pedalling was also applied to light three and four-wheeled machines. A quadri-cycle was built in 1846, which incorporated means for varying the effective crank length to provide the best advantage for different circumstances of propulsion. However, velocipedes of this type were more novel than useful—only some of them were provided with brakes, and, as they were not suitable for serious travel at night, lamps were not provided.

The twenty years which followed Macmillan's bicycle are a bit of a puzzle, the main reason for this being that they are almost devoid of technical development. The scarcity of records for the period, 1840 to 1860, however, make any accurate assessment difficult. The reason for the puzzle is that the 1860's heralded the debut of the first commercially produced bicycle —the 'boneshaker'. The difference between the boneshaker and the earlier hobby-horse, (and for that matter Macmillan's bicycle); was that it had a crank fitted to the *front* wheel. And at this point it is worth looking back to 1820, and the famous caricature of the Prince Regent lying flat on a draisienne which was mentioned earlier. In his attempt to make the machine as ridiculous as possible, the artist had drawn cranks and pedals attached to the front wheel! What had been conceived as satire had become reality—not an uncommon occurrence when one remembers George Orwell, Jules Verne, and Kafka. Obviously some underground activity had been going on between 1840 and 1860, and in spite of the anonymity which insists in cloaking the whole thing in a fog, two key names again emerge.

The place is Paris and the two names which are always bracketed with the earliest boneshaker are those of Pierre Michaux and Pierre Lallement. Michaux was a manufacturer of perambulators and three-wheeled velocipedes and in his workshop employed Lallement, who was a mechanic. But this is where the fog enters into the story a little, and dates and accounts become confused. In 1863 Lallement is reputed to have fitted pedals to the front wheel of a hobby-horse. Controversy still rages among the enthusiasts on this point, and the truth is still not known, if it ever will be. What is significant is that controversy raged at the time also, and not without reason, either. For it was around about this time that people began to realise the potential of the commercial exploitation of the new innovation. If not bare-faced avarice, then one of the milder forms of that side of human nature began to assert itself! It is possible that Lallement did make some major contribution to the idea, and that Michaux later developed it into the form that was known in England as the boneshaker.

However, writing in 1893, Henry Michaux, a son of Pierre, gave his own account of the attaching of the famous pedals to the hobby-horse. He asserted that, in 1861, a customer brought a hobby-horse to the Michaux workshop for repair. Michaux, and another son, Ernest, considered the problem for a while. Then the father suggested that a cranked axle should be fitted to the hub of the front wheel, 'like the crank-handle of a grindstone' so that it could be turned by the feet of the rider. And this, says Henry, is just what Ernest did, if not immediately, then a few weeks later. Whatever the truth is, the national monument erected to the memory of Pierre and Ernest Michaux at Bar-le-Duc officially recognises them as the 'inventeurs et propagateurs du vélocipède a pédale.' But staunch upholders of the underdog claim that Lallement, because he was so poor, sold all his ideas to his master for the extra cash. There certainly must have been a lot of hot argument about the whole thing, for, soon after the Michaux bicycle began to be produced in quantity, Lallement left the firm in great dissatisfaction at the general lack of recognition for his part in the invention. In 1866 he went to America, where, in association with a James Carrol of Ausonia, Connecticut, he took out the first patent for a bicycle to be granted in that country.

Some bitterness must have remained, for he returned to Paris just before the great Paris Exhibition of 1867. The bicycle was just beginning to be generally adopted in France, and Lallement started a company of his own to compete with Michaux. The business must not have thrived, for the year 1896, when he was nearing the end of his days, found him back in the States working for the Pope Manufacturing Company.

But the Michauxs' of Paris blazed away! No time for argument and bad-tempered mechanics. No time for petty squabbles. No time for internicine strife. There was money to be made. This was the time of the steam engine, the railways, and the great flush of mechanical inventions in other fields. Today's dream could become tomorrow's fortune. This was the time of the *nouveau riche*. And the *nouveau riche* contributed to the popularity of the new bicycle, the boneshaker. The wheel had turned a full circle, and the French once more led the world in the bicycle field.

The Michaux firm produced two machines in 1861, one hundred and forty-two machines in 1862, and by 1865 their annual production was more than four hundred machines.

Three years later a new factory which employed three hundred workmen, was built near the Arc de Triomphe. Pierre and Ernest continued in business until 1869, by which time the boneshaker was well established in France. Then they sold their interest in the firm for two hundred thousand francs to a family called Oliver, who traded as the Compagnie Parisienne. The dream had become a fortune!

Other manufacturing firms sprang up and mushroomed in Paris and elsewhere in France. As well as the Olivers, names such as Tribout and Meyer of Paris, Truffault of Tours, and Rosseau of Marseilles became synonymous with the bicycle. The name of Meyer in particular should be noted, for he is reputed to have built in 1869, at the suggestion of clockmaker André Guilmet, the first chain-driven safety bicycle. Ball bearings were applied to front wheel spindles by J. Suriray, and were later improved on by James Moore, an Englishman living in France at the time and who is also reputed to have won the first ever cycle race which was held in Paris in 1868.

The technical advances made by the French was admirably illustrated by the first ever cycle show, held at the Pré-Catalan, Paris, in November, 1869. Featured at the show were machines with light all-metal construction, wheels with wire spokes, tubular frames, solid rubber tyres, front wheel brakes, spring-mounted front wheels, mudguards, and even primitive forms of freewheel devices and change-speed gears. These advances would not surprise a child today, but it must be remembered that the motor-car had yet to come, and the bicycle, therefore, was the catalyst of technical innovation, both major and minor. For instance, the mass production of the bicycle for a widening market actually sparked off the mass production of ball bearings in the 1870's. What is certain is that the exhibits at the first cycle show in 1869 probably had the same effect on onlookers as the latest shiny monsters at the motor shows have on the young, and not-so-young tyros of today. They probably discussed the solid rubber tyre with the same mixture of awe and enthusiasm which greets the latest super-charged sports car today.

It is almost a weary truism that war always provides a spurt to the development of technology, and industry in particular. In its perverted way, war did exactly the opposite in France. The outbreak of the Franco-Prussian War in 1870 put a sudden stop to further development. Although the threads were picked up after the war, the pause gave other countries a chance to catch up with the French. And England, especially, was not slow to grasp the opportunity, as will be seen.

Johnson's Pedestrian Hobbyhorse Riding School, at 337 Strand, and 40 Brewer Street, Golden Square, London. Drawn by H. Alken and published April 17, 1819. (See Chapter 1)

Johnson's Hobbyhorse. 1818. One of the first bicycles. (See Chapter 1). Probably copied from the French or German models of around the same period

2

'WALKING IS ON ITS LAST LEGS'

A young Englishman called Rowley Turner, who was studying in Paris in 1866, had just been appointed Paris agent for the Coventry Sewing Machine Company. Being a period when nepotism was taken for granted, it is not surprising to find out that his uncle, Josiah Turner was general manager of the said company. Nepotism or not, it turned out to be quite a fortuitious move. For young Rowley not only had his wits about him, but in the same year took a great interest in a boneshaker which someone had brought along to the gymnasium which he used. Interest mounted to enthusiasm and Rowley mounted a boneshaker of his own, the result being that he became an expert rider. The Paris Exhibition of 1867 more than likely increased his interest and gave him a chance of inspecting the new French machines at close quarters.

The first cycle race has already been mentioned. Held in May of 1868 over a distance of 1,200 metres, it probably set Rowley Turner's head awhirl with ideas, for he arrived in England six months later with one of the latest Michaux bicycles. He arrived at Coventry by rail, and caused a sensation by riding the strange machine from the station to the works of the Coventry Sewing Machine Company at Cheylesmore. He caused a further surprise when he produced an order for four hundred machines for export to France. Aided by his Uncle Josiah, and by the fact that the sewing machine business had been getting slack lately, he persuaded the company to take on the order. The minutes of the Coventry Sewing Machine Company of February 15, 1869 include the following item:

'The directors have received an order for a large number of velocipedes and the manufacture of them *not* being in accordance with the articles of association, the Proprietors will be asked to sanction manufacture'.

The result was that the name of the company was changed to Coventry Machinists Company Limited, and production of the bicycles commenced. Later the same year, enterprising lad that he was, Rowley gained publicity by riding a velocipede in a race at Crystal Palace, London. Unfortunately, just as the first consignment was ready for shipping to France, the Franco-Prussian War broke out. The order was cancelled. In fact, Rowley Turner was in France at the time and had been caught in the seige of Paris. The last train had left, and he escaped on his Michaux bicycle!

There was no alternative for the Coventry Machinists but to develop the home market. And here again Rowley Turner, safely back in England, showed great initiative in securing orders in London. He took part in many long distance rides, and capped them all by eventually riding his boneshaker from London to Brighton. The future of the bicycle in England was assured. Thus was born the Coventry cycle industry, which not only boosted the commercial life of the city, but eventually made it the centre of the world's cycle industry.

No mention of Coventry would be complete without mention of one of her most famous figures—James Starley. Starley worked for the Coventry Sewing Machine Company as general foreman, under Josiah Turner, and was an extremely inventive man in his own right. As soon as the company started to manufacture their first boneshakers, he started making improvements in the design. His first action had been to lift the Michaux with his own hands. 'Too heavy and cumbersome,' was his first criticism. So, he started making it lighter and easier to handle. Again, the usual practice among riders of the day was to take a short run and leap into the saddle of the machine. Starley fitted a step to the hub of the rear wheel, the significance of which becomes clear when one reads the following extract from a journal of 1869:

'There are those who sneer at the new fangled carriages and point out that similar machines have been tried before, and, for practical use have been found woefully wanting. They predict sprains, ruptures, dislocations, and death as the penalty of using these mechanical contrivances.'

One can practically smell the fire and brimstone in this piece of Victorian anti-bicycle evangelism. The evangelist, one feels, would not in the least be convinced by Starley's step improvement. By all accounts, though, our evangelist might even claim some justification, for they must have been monstrous machines to mount. Writing in 1892, a Rev. G. Herbert gives an account of riding a 1867 velocipede (probably a Michaux model):

'It was very wonderful to us, but very different from the beautifully finished machines we see in the present day. The wheels were nearly of a size, about 36 inches high; the felloes were of iron, flat like those of a waggon; there were no rubber tyres, and though to us then it seemed to go with the greatest of ease, it made a mighty rattle, needing no warning bell to tell the unwary pedestrian of its approach. Now, mounting and dismounting in those days was a different thing from mounting a modern machine. In the "ordinary" modern machine, (the writer is here referring to a penny-farthing type bicycle, which would have been modern in his day) the rider put the machine in motion, holding the handles, and then simply lifts himself into the saddle by the aid of the little step close to the hind wheel. But in those old machines, the saddle was too far forward and the machine too long to make that possible. The method we had to adopt was a different one, and mounting was the worst part of the whole process. If I had not been used to the vaulting horse in Germany, I do not think I should have succeeded in this part of the process. Grasping the handles, we set off at a fast run, keeping alongside the machine till we got considerable momentum on it, then we vaulted into the saddle. This required practice and agility, but the spice of danger in it simply added to the zest with which I set about mastering it. After sundry scratches, many bruises, and with the expenditure of much unnecessary exertion, I at last mastered the art and was not a little proud of my accomplishment. Of course, these early machines were merely toys, for we used to think eleven or twelve miles a good ride. The labour was considerable and the chafing excessive. A railway bridge or a very slight rise in the ground brought us to a standstill.'

At least the Rev. Herbert was all for giving the boneshaker a chance. Others were not so open-minded, and some were even violently against the whole idea. A London journalist of the time expressed himself unequivocally:

'We think they ought to be excluded from London parks also. Surely a sufficient infliction is placed upon the irate mortality by the introduction of the perambulator, without endangering life and limb still more by allowing velocipeditation.'

That word 'also' in the first sentence has an ominous ring about it. Heaven only knows what the fellow would have written if he had known that Parliament was also busying itself with the application of the boneshaker to the day-to-day administration of the country. On the 13th of May, 1869, Mr Charles Hambro, M.P. for Weymouth, asked the Post Master General in Parliament 'if it is a fact that in certain parts of Wales, the Post Office mails are not conveyed on velocipedes instead of horses, and if this change has been found to add to the efficiency and economy of the service.'

In part of his reply, the Post Master General, the Marquis of Hartington said: 'An experiment has been tried or will shortly be tried, to ascertain whether in certain rural districts these machines can be used by Post messengers on roads which are not very hilly, or are otherwise adapted for the purpose.'

Today's rural postman on his bicycle is, no doubt, the outcome of these experiments. If the Marquis of Hartington had heard about M. Dreuze's experiments of 40 years previously, he certainly was not going to be daunted by their failure.

The late 1860's were, of course, the days of the equal wheel sized velocipedes—the glorious penny-farthing had yet to come. And, although cycling was gaining ground as a pastime, there was still enough opposition to the recreation to make the protagonists include serious social justification in their arguments. A writer at the time reported their position thus:

'The velocipedists urge that when velocipeding was introduced a generation ago, it was the fashion to decry muscular exertion, and to elevate mental improvement, until our clerks and shopkeepers were pale and indolent dyspeptics instead of vigorous and healthy members of the human family. If the velocipede only popularises bodily exercise among the sedentary class, no one will affirm that their mission is a fruitless one.'

With only minor changes in the wording, exactly the same argument has been proffered to the pot-bellied, car-driving executives of today. In an amazing anticipation of the use to which the 'Provos' of Holland have put their white bicycles, the same writer also offered the following thoughts:

'There are enthusiasts who see in the bicycle the solution of some gnarled social problem, and believe that a tricycle will obviate some festering evil of our era, though at present the popular toy of the hour only flatters our pride by giving power over space.'

At this time, calling the bicycle a 'popular toy' was misleading, for, not only was it firmly established in France, but it was also sweeping England and America. In spite of the fact that prices were still steep enough to keep them out of the hands of the toiling masses, they were selling like hot cakes to the wealthier classes.

One American journalist even went as far as to exclaim in his column: 'Walking is on its last legs!' In quoting this, no reproach is intended to the well-known American gift of exaggeration. Although an overstatement, it caught the mood of the time. Another writer of the period informs us:

'We are told by some enthusiastic manufacturers that the management of the velocipede is now a part of every liberal education, and to a certain extent is treated as such in America and France.'

Some adventurous people must have been experimenting with the styles of riding, for the writer continues to warn:

'But the art is sufficiently delicate, and the position of the rider sufficiently absurd without being made more so absurd by any gymnastic performances.'

And sure enough, one newspaper report tells us that:

'One genius is already preparing to velocipede himself across Niagara in a groove-wheeled machine, and other semi-insane mortals exhibit at once their foolhardiness and their ambition by riding along the parapet of the Seine. It may be hoped if there be any real merit in the invention, that the public will not be deterred from appreciating it, because of the acrobatic performances of these velocipedomaniacs.'

How dull the word 'cyclist' sounds compared with that last one! The acrobatics of these velocipedomaniacs gave rise to some glorious speculation on the part of another writer. Giving vent to his imagination, he went so far as to propose a bicycle-based aeroplane!

'We shall, no doubt, have such a machine calculated to carry fifty or even a thousand people, driven by steam, and we may also have the apparatus constructed for one, so that the ardent lover may set at nought the bolts and bars of an angry father, and fly to the balcony of his inamorata, or even plan an elopement from her very casement.'

Then comes the stern warning (remember this was written in 1869):

'But the invention of a flying machine would be a serious evil indeed, in many ways, for the world. And, yet, we are continually told that we are on the threshold of it. We are periodically startled by paragraphs in *The Times* intimating the approach of some Yankee through the air, or announcing the advancing completion of an apparatus that will carry us to China in 24 hours.'

That, however, is a far cry from the bicycle. By 1870 velocipeding, or cycling, as it was later to be known, was again in full swing. But unlike the 1820's, this time it was being taken a lot more seriously. In America even art galleries were being turned into gymnasia for the teaching of the cycling art. An English chronicler of 1870 tell us that:

'. . . in Liverpool the gymnasia are crowded nightly by expectant riders. Manchester has caught the fever. Birmingham has caught the symptoms. London is talking about the new excitement. The watering places are grateful for the new sensation, and embryo riders exclaim—

I shall have no horse to feed,
For I ride on a velocipede.

The writers of those days had certainly little to learn from present-day advertising copywriters in the use of superlatives. The craze, however, was not without its marital dangers. Goodness knows how many marriages were broken up by the wanton, albeit unconscious behaviour of the husband described in this rather despairing letter by an American wife to the Binghampton Republic in the year 1860:

'. . . he goes out in the day-time and rides a velocipede, and then keeps up the propelling motion with his feet all night. I don't like it . . .'

It was another American who produced the following absurd but hilarious definition of velocipede:

Viel (German) Hoss (English) Pied (French)
Translation: 'Much-hoss-afoot'.

The developments and improvements which took place in a period of a few years was notable, even by today's standards. Rubber packings were used for saddles and footrests: crude wire spokes were introduced in 1866; the slotted crank for adjusting the length of the 'push' was developed by the Hanlon brothers in America; and the front (driving) wheel began to get larger to improve performance and riding comfort. And, the earliest recorded instance of the use of rubber tyres on a bicycle, was in 1868, when J. Hastings rode a boneshaker fitted with tyres of solid rubber. Carrying out a test, he rode over 30 miles on snow-covered roads. In the same year, in America, a Rev. Mr Edwards of Chicago also used solid rubber tyres on a boneshaker. Previously, these bicycles had been fitted with iron tyres, usually over wooden wheels. One can imagine that the iron-shod bicycle properly deserved the name 'boneshaker'. The attendant noise is well suggested in the following verse:

'Bring me the bells, the rattle bring,
And bring the hobby I bestrode,
When pleased, in many a sportive ring,
Around the room I jovial rode.'

The friction between Lallement and Michaux has already been mentioned. In 1866, when Lallement went to America in disgust, *Scientific American* recorded a patent for a two-wheel velocipede, known as Lallement's patent, but no one appeared to take any notice of the fact; besides which they were still, in that year, regarded as a fashionable French toy. When, however, it became obvious that there was a lot of money to be made, a Mr Calvin Witty, of Broadway, NY, went quietly to ascertain how manufacture could be controlled. He found the holders of patents and bought the exclusive rights of manufacturing of treadles and grinding arms in the USA. Witty then informed all the manufacturers. They were upset but pooh-poohed his claims and laughed at the notices. However, they soon found that the law was on Witty's side, and they all eventually paid up. It would not be America if some wild claims did not spring from the fertile imaginations of the citizens of that country. In 1866 a Mr Stephen Smith of New York claimed to have invented the bicycle and later introduced it into France!

3

THE FRONT WHEEL GROWS LARGER

At this point in its history, the bicycle takes on a radically new shape. The front wheel grows larger and the back wheel smaller, and it becomes what is for most people the symbol of the bicycle for all time—the pennyfarthing. Some enthusiasts grow hot under the collar at the use of the word 'pennyfarthing', and prefer the term 'ordinary' or grand old ordinary, or simply 'GOO'. It is interesting to trace the development of the big front wheel. And here the French led again. The Michaux type of boneshaker continued to be made and used until about 1872. It had begun to decline in popularity before that, however, mainly because of the amount of energy needed to propel its heavy structure. Sad to say, that, after 1870 the boneshaker was relegated to the status of a learner's machine, and models could be bought for as little as a pound or two. Nowadays collectors pay as much as a hundred pounds or more for a boneshaker.

Improvements and radical changes began to be introduced. But the invention of the pennyfarthing is generally attributed to a Monsieur Magee of Paris, who, in 1869, in Paris, made a machine of steel, iron and rubber with a front or driving wheel of 48 inches and a small trailing or rear wheel of 24 inches. The pennyfarthing had arrived. English manufacturers followed the French lead, and soon, ordinarys of all types were being designed, built and ridden with enthusiasm. Riders liked them, because, not only were they a challenge to skill, with their high riding seats, but they also gave quite high average road speeds.

Names which are now household in England began to make the new type of bicycle with a will: The Coventry Machinists Company and Starley and Smith and Hillman in Coventry. Starley produced so many improvements for the bicycle, both in general design and in details, that he became known as the 'Father of the Cycle Industry.' Also H. Clark and Dan Rudge of Wolverhampton, and Thomas Humber of Nottingham were making bicycles in small numbers but of excellent quality. In Sheffield, Hydes and Wigfull, a firm of agricultural implement makers turned their minds to producing high-class ordinarys. W. H. J. Grout produced his progressive 'Tension' bicycle and also made tricycles. John Keen, of Surbiton, built machines lighter and taller than had been thought possible. These were the beginnings of the English bicycle industry, which was eventually to become famous throughout the world. By 1874, there were some twenty firms making bicycles in England; Henry Sturmey's publication, *The Indispensable Bicyclist's Handbook* (1879), lists about three hundred different machines made by some sixty firms, mostly in Coventry, Birmingham and London, but others in Brighton, Cheltenham and King's Lynn.

But, although M. Magee of Paris is generally recognised as the inventor of the pennyfarthing, English inventors at the same time were not without their own ideas. Especially W. F. Reynolds and J. A. Mays, the inventors of the 'Phantom' in the year 1869, the same year as Magee's pennyfarthing. The

'Phantom' was a truly radical design—not just an improved Michaux type boneshaker. For a start, it was of a lighter construction (53 lb.) and it had an articulated triangular frame made of light iron rods. It had wooden wheels but with double wire spokes—probably one of the first practical examples of the suspension wheel with tension spokes. Although the suspension wheel as such was patented as far back as 1802 by G. F. Bauer, this was the first time it was used on a bicycle. The following year (1870), James Starley patented his ribbon wheel, which was originally spoked with narrow brass ribbons, the ribbons eventually becoming wire spokes. Soon after that, Starley broke with the Coventry Machinists Company and formed his own company with William Hillman and B. Smith, in St John's Street, Coventry.

And it was here he designed the famous 'Ariel' bicycle, his first pennyfarthing-type machine. Although Starley and Hillman took out a joint patent for the Ariel in 1870, it was not actually put into production until the following year. It was introduced in September 1871 at a price of £8, or, with a speed-gear, £12. The speed-gear, also invented by Starley, made the front wheel revolve at twice the speed as the crank spindle, and is probably the first example of a British speed-gear for use with a bicycle. But before its introduction to the public, William Hillman was very keen on making a spectacular gesture to launch it with the utmost publicity. Finally they decided that both should try something really eye-opening, such as setting up a cycling record together. They decided to attempt the ride from London to Coventry in a single day. And they did.

A contemporary account of their ride tells about it in some detail:

'To demonstrate to the bicycling fraternity the qualities of the new bicycle now being manufactured by Messrs. Starley and Hillman of Coventry, these two gentlemen undertook to ride their machines from London to Coventry within the day. Mr James Starley is well-known as an inventor and is prominent in the sewing-machine industry. Lately he has turned his inventive ability to the improvement of the velocipede. Mr Starley was one of the first to master the art of riding the bicycle, as the modern machines are called, and is often to be seen in the saddle. Mr William Hillman is an enthusiast bicyclist and has taken part in several races. The bicycles are of the latest design with iron-spoked wheels, and rubber tyres and are fitted with Mr Starley's ingenious improvements.

'The two gentlemen took their bicycles by train to Euston Station. spending the night in the Station Hotel. Arranging to be called before daylight, they had a light breakfast and mounted their machines just as the sun was rising. At that hour only the early workers were about to witness the unusual sight of velocipedes speeding through the streets. The cobbled roads caused the bicyclists some discomfiture . . . Once through London, the country roads were smoother and the two bicyclists made good progress, reaching St Alban's at about 8.30 a.m., where they stopped to have an ample breakfast before starting on the most arduous part of the journey.

'Watling Street from St Albans to Dunstable runs over a part of the Chiltern Hills, but the road is well graded and smooth, and although on some of the steeper hills, the bicyclists had to walk, compensation came in the long down-hill portions, and there, so Mr Hillman says, Mr Starley's weight gave great velocity to his machine, a speed of at least twelve miles an hour being attained. Disaster might have overtaken the gentlemen who wished to take full advantage of the hills, had it not been for Mr Starley's ingenious brake.

'By one o'clock the riders had covered nearly half of the distance and halted at an inn near Bletchley to partake of a dinner and to rest for an hour. When they remounted, Mr Starley complained of strain to his leg muscles. From here the condition of the road deteriorated and great care had to be taken to avoid loose stones. They plodded on through Stony Stratford and Towcester, cheered by the inhabitants of towns and villages, few of whom had seen a bicycle.

'Only one mishap befell the adventurous bicyclists—Mr Hillman was thrown from his machine when the rubber tyre of his front wheel came off, but he escaped with nothing worse than a grazed hand. He was able to bind the tyre on again and proceed without further trouble.

'Both gentlemen admitted that the last few miles from Daventry to Coventry daunted them. By this time they were both tired and when night fell there was the added difficulty of avoiding stones and holes in the road, and Mr Starley, who is no longer a young man, admitted that he was near the limit of his endurance before they saw the lights of Coventry and pedalling bravely they reached Mr Starley's residence just as the clock of St Michael's struck the hour.

'This astonishing feat has been acclaimed as a triumph for the bicyclists who completed the journey of ninety-six miles, and for the bicycles which had no mechanical trouble, except for the tyre mishap. It demonstrates that the bicycle that has been developed by Messrs. Starley and Hillman from the velocipede is a most efficient form of human transport. It may be recorded that the two intrepid gentlemen, though tired, and stiff, after their long ride, were no worse for their adventure.'

This gruelling ride put the Ariel on the map. The machine sold well, and in 1873 the previously mentioned Mr J. Moore actually rode 14½ miles in one hour on one of these models. The front wheel was 50 inches in diameter and the back wheel was 14, and the cranks were slotted so that the pedals could be adjusted from a 5-inch radius to a 6½-inch radius.

Another famous bicycle of the same period was the 'Tension' made by the indefatigable W. H. J. Grout. The large wheel of the Tension had the cranks directly connected to the hub, the heads of the radial spokes being clamped by sideplates to the hub flanges. The outer ends of the spokes were threaded and screwed into eyed nipples, loosely riveted to the rim, so that the spoke tension and the true of the wheel could be easily and accurately adjusted. This was the origin of a method which is still used to the present day. Another method of spoking a wheel, and which is also in current use, was invented by James Starley at the same time. After two years of experiment, Starley took out a patent for his tangent-spoke wheel. Previously the common practice had been to make wheels with spokes radiating straight from the hub to the outer rim. But Starley perfected a method of setting the spokes at a slant so that they crossed each other at an angle. This method has never been bettered and, in fact, survives today in cycles and motorcycles.

By the early 1870's, the enthusiasm for road racing had grown to considerable proportions. To demonstrate the growing possibilities of the new high wheel machines as practical road vehicles, James Sparrow, a bicycle manufacturer of London, organised a fantastic bicycle ride. He set up and financed four riders who travelled on Grout Tension bicycles from London to John O'Groats in fifteen days. The increased interest in the machines on the part of both maker and user, led to more and more improvements. The front wheel got larger and larger until it was limited only by the height of the rider and the length of his legs. Had Finn McCool wanted a penny-farthing, one would have been made for him! Makers further reduced the weight by improved techniques, such as hollow frames and forks. Ball bearings for the spindles made for easier running. It has already been pointed out that the mass production of ball bearings was brought about by the growing output of bicycles.

The ladies were not to be left out either. During 1874, the Starley organisation produced a special ladies' model of the Ariel machine. It was a peculiar machine, by all accounts, and never became popular, which is not surprising when one reads a description of it. As was befitting a staunch and true Victorian, Starley designed the machine around women's clothes of the period, instead of suggesting that women's clothes be modified to suit the bicycle, God forbid! It incorporated certain features based on an earlier boneshaker design of S. W. Thomas. The female rider sat in a side-saddle position, the handlebars being shortened on one side and lengthened on the other. The rear wheel was mounted on an overhung axle and the front wheel was offset from the track of the rear wheel, to counteract the bias of the side-saddle position. It must have been the very devil to balance and operate, and was one of

Starley's few failures. It was saved by converting it into a tricycle by adding a small wheel on one side of the large front wheel. Finally, it ended up as the Coventry Lever Tricycle.

But if the ladies' Ariel was unstable, then the gentlemen's model was only a little less so. This was so unstable compared with the modern safety bicycle that it became almost a cult 'thing' to be seen riding a grand old ordinary even when it had passed out of fashion and had been superseded by the 'safety'. So strong was the cult that a number of cyclists continued to use the ordinary right into the 1890's. But the danger of taking a 'header' was always prevalent. This is perhaps best illustrated by a story current in the 1890's. It seems that the Shah of Persia visited a cycle works during a visit to the United Kingdom. He bought a couple of the grand old ordinarys and shipped them to Persia for his personal use. His attempts to ride them failed miserably, so—after being cursed as Contraptions of the Evil One—the GOO's were cast aside. Some time afterwards, an unusual amount of bickering and fighting took place among the ladies of the Harem which the regular means of punishment failed to abate. So the machines were brought out and the turbulent ladies were placed on them and pushed off on their way. Amid screams and protestations, they fell off. The number of times they were compelled to tumble was regulated by the enormity of their crimes.

The dangers of the pennyfarthing are perhaps even better illustrated by this piece from a cycling magazine of the late 1870's:

> 'When a man is riding a bicycle he looks neither to the right nor to the left, but appears to be gazing about five hundred yards into futurity, as if trying to solve the problems of the hereafterness of the unknowableness of the unknowable hereafter. He is not, however. He is simply wondering, in case of a sudden header, whether his skull would be split open wide, or if he would escape with his nose mashed all over his face.'

No wonder the pennyfarthing became a cult. But the ulti-

Above, Kirkpatrick Macmillan's bicycle of 1839. This is a copy of the bicycle on which Macmillan committed the first ever recorded cycling offence. (See Chapter 1). *Below,* The original Michaux bicycle of 1865. This was the machine which really started the bicycle boom of the 1860's. (See Chapter 2)

The 'Ariel' pennyfarthing of 1870. Made by James Starley, it was one of the first pennyfarthings in existence. (See Chapter 3)

mate danger is probably best underlined by this report which appeared in the *Daily Mail* of the 4th of May, 1896. It is datelined Largs, Scotland and the machine is obviously a grand old ordinary:

'A shocking bicycle fatality has occurred near Largs, Ayrshire. The town is approached by a zig-zag declivity, along which a young man named Wardrobe, of Glasgow, was riding yesterday, when his machine became unmanageable, owing to the steepness of the descent, and dashed with such terrible violence into the solid rock, through which the road is cut, that the rider's neck was broken and his body otherwise much lacerated. Death was instantaneous.'

That tells us as much about the journalistic styles of the day as about the dangers of riding an ordinary.

Before the advent of the modern safety model, some people gave thought to the safety problems connected with the ordinary. In America, one gentleman thought of a bright stroke to stabilise the machine—he put the big wheel at the back and the little one at the front. The pedals were still connected to the big wheel, but now the little wheel was the steering wheel. This model was known as the 'Star'. It could not have worked too well, for it was short-lived. However, it is said that an Irishman, on seeing the model for the first time, exclaimed: 'Be God, sir, the big wheel is the little wheel, and the back wheel is in the front!'

But the cult remained strong. Writing in the 1880's, one enthusiast could hardly contain himself about the pleasures of the ordinary:

'The motion of the ordinary was more exhilarating than that of the "safety". The position, so nicely balanced, nearly on one wheel; the absence of a wheel to be pushed in front, wheelbarrow fashion; the free, billowy, rolling motion that ensued, gave to riding and coasting on it a peculiar charm that was wholly its own, and afforded sensations which those who have enjoyed them count as among the most beautiful of their lives.'

Such dedication derives from a blind faith which gives birth to either the crank or the genius. The choice of category into which the author of the above falls is sensibly left to the reader.

Directions and lessons for riding the pennyfarthing, however, abounded at the time. Here is an extract from one of them:

'Should you still fancy yourself falling over on either side, turn the wheel *the same way that your body inclines*, and you will be able to proceed as before. This turning of the wheel in the direction of the falling Bicycle is the grand secret.'

Apparently, if you did happen to fall from a pennyfarthing, the other grand secret was to swing your legs around the front fork and land with your both feet on the ground, the fork between them. If nothing else, the Victorian cyclists must have been brilliant acrobats! (If the reader considers the above instructions on riding a little ludicrous, then let him ponder this: the author has in his possession a two-page colour advertisement from a New Zealand literary magazine published in 1946, which proclaims and proudly presents a book for the price of 5 shillings, entitled *'How to Ride a Bicycle in Seventeen Lovely Colours'*.)

The instruction on riding continues with encouragement for the beginner:

'I do not believe in the man who becomes a fair rider at his first attempt. In this, as in everything else, perseverance is indispensable. Never forget that failure is the mother of success.'

That last glorious epigram is the first outrageous cousin, no doubt, of the other famous epigram, 'Necessity is the mother of invention'. It sounds rather like an extreme case of chewing more than you bite off.

Of course the big front wheel led to some splendid hybrid animals, such as the monocycle. One of these is recorded as having been patented by a certain Elisha Dyer and Allen Green of Rhode Island, USA, in 1869. A rather restrained contemporary description of the machine runs as follows:

'The most reasonable of these unreasonable things is constructed as follows: Wheel diameter, 8 feet upwards; broad axle, at least 3 feet broad; the passenger sits inside the wheel, on the axle, and works the whole thing by treadles and cranks. A thick iron tyre binds the whole thing together.'

Speeds claimed for this monster varied between thirty and forty miles per hour. The description continues:

'It is clear that if he did not keep his head quite erect, he would be liable to be caught by the revolving spokes, he would probably be either beheaded without trial or gradually reduced to pulp. There is no brake either, so that, if the wheel got started downhill, and did not meet with a railway embankment or anything equally formidable to check its wild career, it would probably go on for an unlimited distance, and carry the poor man in its interior, in much the same way that the historical leg of Myneer Van Clam carried off—and, according to German legend still does,—its wretched owner.'

None of these were ever popular, and there is no record of one of them having been ridden for any distance. Not surprising, as, no doubt, people at that time were averse to being broken on a wheel. An American writer probably summed it up best when he said, at the time: 'It would be as easy to keep upright on such a wheel, as it is to sit on a chair balanced on two legs, upon the rather uncertain substratum of a slack rope.' The same American writer seemed not only to be a wit but also to be quite anti-cycling in totality. For he also described the boneshaker of a few years previous in the following acid terms:

'Riding a true-story Indian hog just turned loose to fat on beech nuts would be sweet cream in comparison with this invention. Sliding downhill on a hand-saw, tooth side up, would be two degrees more comfortable than experimenting on one of these contrivances.'

Perhaps the best story illustrating the difficulty of riding a pennyfarthing is the one told about that old campaigner, playwright and genius, George Bernard Shaw. Shaw was spending the weekend with Sidney and Beatrice Webb at their country home. While out walking (one of his enthusiasms) he discovered another of his enthusiasms, an old pennyfarthing, in an outhouse. Delighted, he took the bicycle to the top of a hill near the house, and proceeded to ride it down the hill at great speed. Being a tall man, he could handle the pennyfarthing very well.

Sidney Webb spotted Shaw through the window at his fun and games, and ran out of the house, bent on joining the frolic. He danced up and down, joyful as a child. 'Let me have a go! Let me have a go!', he cried to Shaw. Now, Shaw had more than a streak of mischievousness in him, and his eyes glinted with devilment at the sight of Webb. He knew full well that Webb was far too small a man to handle a pennyfarthing. So he encouraged Webb to have a go, his mind savouring the vision of him coming a cropper down the hill.

But he had reckoned without Webb's wife, Beatrice. A stern and over-serious woman, she caught sight of Shaw just as he was helping Sidney into the saddle. She dashed out of the house and admonished both of them for what no doubt she regarded as their flippancy. Sending Sidney back into the house to continue his work on the history of something or other, she left Shaw fuming at having been thwarted by a woman. He no doubt pondered on the irony of an enlightened woman regarding as a flippancy a machine which had done so much for female emancipation. One can imagine him muttering into his ginger beard, 'Abolish the pound, but preserve the pennyfarthing'.

But perhaps it is too easy today to stress the awkwardness of the big wheel ordinary bicycle. After all, not only was it ridden with gusto at the time, but it led to the development of the tricycle, and the founding of cycling clubs all over the British Isles as well as the Continent. For, by the late 1870's and the early 1880's, Britain had once more gained the title as the leading cycling country of the world. There was, no doubt, a great deal of cross-pollination between the enthusiasts and the flourishing bicycle industry in Coventry and elsewhere. Incidentally, first the prominence and then the eclipse of cycling throughout the Western World in the nineteenth century can be quite bewildering. In one period France leads, then it is the turn of Germany, then the British Isles, then the USA, then France again, and so on. If one remembers that Von Drais (a German) was one of the key names in the history of the bicycle so far, the following extract from an English cycling magazine of 1879 has a particular irony:

'The machines most in vogue in the country (Germany) are those manufactured by the Howe Machine Co., a make little known among English club men, while specimens of the well-known "Challenge", "Coventry Machinists", "Rudge", and "Premier", are frequently found. There is no bicycle manufactory in Germany, one started in Dortmund not having succeeded.'

But this was, according to the same writer, being put right very fast:

'Favoured by good roads, beautiful scenery, and a more equable climate than that of England, bicycling has now taken firm root as one of the sports of German youth, and I anticipate that in a few years' time, it will attain to such proportions as to be regarded there, as at home here, as the national sport of the country. Riders will go further and further afield every time they mount, clubs will come into existence in all the towns, the small (here the writer means a front wheel of 48 inches diameter!) and usually old machines will be discarded for fair-sized machines and roadsters of modern manufacture, and in ten or twelve years' time, England will have to look to her laurels and bestir herself to maintain her proud position as the first bicycling country of the world.'

The last-mentioned position is probably held by France to-day. Nonetheless, cycling hit an unprecedented peak around the early 1880's in England. And so did the tricycle. Nowadays we tend to think of the tricycle as a child's toy, but in those days it was ridden by adults who possibly thought the ordinary too unstable. Again, this sudden popularity is well documented. A contemporary magazine notes:

'Reference to a "sociable" tricycle calls to mind the stupendous growth of the use of these machines during the present season, undoubtedly traceable, to a great extent, to the splendid show made of the three-wheelers at the last Stanley Exhibition, whilst recent performances on double tricycles, such as that of the "Bairn and the Boy on the Acton bus", accomplishing 59 miles in seven hours, and of *"Jarge primus et Jarge secundus"*—two lengthy Cicestrians—on the Finchley TC bus, running 70 miles without an effort in 10 hours, shows that these convenient machines are not so much inferior to the bicycle, in point of speed, as their apparent cumbrousness would lead you to expect.'

The references to the 'Bairn and the Boy' and the two Jarges are obviously the nicknames of well-known cycling personalities of the time. The popularity of the tricycle must have been further increased when that venerable monarch Queen Victoria bought one for the Royal household in 1881. The story of how it came about goes as follows. While holidaying at Osborne on the Isle of Wight, the Queen went out for her regular afternoon drive by horse-drawn coach. Suddenly she sat bolt upright in the open coach—for, ahead of the coach was a young lady on wheels, a tricycle, in fact. At that particular moment the young lady happened to look over her shoulder, probably on hearing the sound of the Queen's carriage. On seeing the Royal coach, she was thrown into something of a panic, for she immediately bent forward and began to pedal away for all her worth. The distance between the coach and the tricycle steadily increased until eventually the young lady outpaced the thing and was never overtaken. Doubtless, the sight of a great flashing mass of spokes and wheels being ridden by a young woman intrigued the Queen. Someone in the Royal household identified the young woman as a Miss Roach, and further enlightened the monarch as to who she was. Her father, a highly respected resident, was, it seems, responsible for introducing these weird machines to the Isle of Wight, where they were becoming all the rage. The machine in question was, in fact, the 'Salvo Quad', a product of Starley Brothers of Coventry. Roach was the sole agent for the Starleys in the Isle. Shortly after, Miss Roach was commanded to give a private demonstration to Queen Victoria of the new machine, in the seclusion of the grounds of Osborne House. The redoubtable monarch wanted to have a close look at the thing at close quarters. She must have been pleased, for she placed an immediate order for one of the 'Salvos', with a Royal Command that James Starley should attend the delivery of the machine in person. Starley records the meeting in a letter to his wife:

'. . . Mr Roach met me off the boat and drove me to Osborne House in his trap. One of Her Majesty's gentlemen was ready waiting for me and was very kind. He told me what to do and how to address the Queen. It seems funny but you must not say thank you to her. You have to say, I am very honoured, Ma'am. He told me that as it was such a nice day Her Majesty would receive me on the lawn, and when we got outside, there she was sitting on a rug on a small garden chair by a round table that was covered with boxes, reading papers with someone who must have been her secretary, I think. Two of her Indian servants were standing nearby and one of her ladies just behind her. I could see the tricycle under a tree and a lady and gentleman looking at it. My gentleman told me to wait a minute where I was, and he went up to the Queen and bowed. She looked up and said something and he backed away a few paces and came to fetch me. He told me to stop when he did and to bow when he presented me which I did. She is a tiny little old lady but somehow you don't think of it when she is talking to you and her voice is deeper than you would expect.

'She said, We are very interested in your tricycle Mr Starley. The Prince Leopold thinks he may soon be able to ride one. You see His Royal Highness examining it now. And then he came over to stand by the Queen and she said to him, this is Mr Starley who invented the tricycle and he was most pleasant and asked questions about my other inventions. Then the Queen said, We believe you have sons working with you Mr Starley and that is very nice for you. Good children are a great support in life. We hope Mrs Starley enjoys good health. Then the lady-in-waiting handed her a little leather case and she held it out to me saying We wish you to have this memento of your visit to Us.

'I was quite overcome and bowed so low that I nearly toppled over as I said I am very honoured, Ma'am. Then the gentleman led me away, and I was very surprised and pleased when the Prince came along and asked me to explain the working of the tricycle to him. A servant was wheeling it behind. We found a nice level drive where I got on and was soon rolling along in fine style. He seemed very pleased with it and thanked me very kindly . . .'

It is quite clear that this action of Queen Victoria gave tricycling a tremendous boost, although it is not recorded if she herself actually rode the thing. It also gave rise to a great deal of snobbery. The Bicycle Touring Club had been formed at Harrogate in 1878, and later became the Cyclists Touring Club, which still exists today. Now, the tricyclists, not having a club of their own at the time, naturally became members of the BTC. They were not too happy with the cyclists they met in the BTC, it seems. For, early in 1882 the following circular was secretly sent to certain members of the BTC with the injunction: Please do not show this to your consul unless you think he is sure to join us.

'It is desired by most Tricyclists to separate themselves entirely from the Bicyclists, who are a disgrace to the pastime, while Tricycling includes Princes, Princesses, Dukes, Earls etc. There are none of the upper circles who ride Bicycles. This is easily seen, and it is plain that the Tricyclists are altogether a better class than the Bicyclists, and require better accommodation on tours etc. A new Tricycling Union has been formed, and could not that body make itself a Tricycle Touring Club as well? This would give a greater advantage over the Bicyclists, who have two different bodies to do the work.'

For sheer priggishness, that takes some beating. However, tricycling eventually lost its popularity and the Tricycling Touring Club died the death. But before leaving the subject it is probably worth mentioning the undisputedly greatest tricyclist who ever lived. His name was Bidlake, and in 1893 he set up a paced, 24-hour record of over 410 miles that still stood even after 1945. He first thought of the unpaced time trial on the road. He devoted his life to cycling and is said not to have suffered fools gladly. Known affectionately as 'Biddy', he died in 1933. There is a monument to him, in the form of a memorial garden, at Girtford Bridge, on the North Road, which he probably knew when it was little better than a footpath. An equally fitting memorial to his name is the following story recounted by a cyclist in 1957. Apparently he had been cycling in the Midlands the year before (1956), and stayed at lodgings for the night. He thought he had struck it lucky when his landlady mentioned that she was used to 'racing cyclists' ways'. Sure enough, at crack of dawn, she produced his breakfast—three raw eggs in a pint of stout! A startled inquiry elicited the information that her racing gentleman always had eggs in stout for breakfast. 'And who was the last racing gentleman to stay here?' she was asked. 'The last', she mused, 'I think . . . yes . . . I'm almost sure . . . it must have been Mr Bidlake.'

4

BRUSHES WITH THE LAW

'I have seen a new cushion pedal, invented by Mr Crooke, of the bicycle agency, Praed Street, Paddington. It seems a useful sort of thing, and is intended to save the owner the great wear of the boot.'

Thus reported the cyclists' equivalent of today's motoring journalist in 1882. Cycling now even had its own newspapers. An advertisement for one of these in an 1881 magazine runs:

'The Cyclist can always be obtained at 152 Fleet Street, every Wednesday morning, after eight a.m. The Cyclist is now unquestionably at the head of the Cycling papers, and is well worthy of the proud position.'

Cycling was now the big sport. But it was not all smooth going. Brushes with the law were frequent, since cyclists were still not numerous enough nor strong enough to elicit the respect of the police, and since the pennyfarthings, with their greater speed, were still regarded as dangerous steeds on the road. The most common offence was the soft impeachment of 'riding furiously'. A magazine columnist of 1881 records his views on the subject:

'No well-disposed rider will have much pity for the tricyclists and bicyclists who are being pounced down upon so energetically by the police for riding furiously on the wood paving at the West End, although lovers of truth for truth's sake alone will desire that the active and intelligent constables could be instructed in the rudiments of calculating the pace of bodies in motion, a science of which they appear to be deplorably ignorant if we are to judge by the "fifteen miles an hour" average generally sworn to. Exaggeration notwithstanding it is pretty evident that this long expanse of wood paving is infested by a hoard of inconsiderate fellows who really do ride at an excessive speed—for the locality—and for the credit of our sport these summonses are looked upon, at the other end of London at least, with equanimity flavoured, I am afraid, by a certain complacent feeling of satisfaction, brought on by the reflections that the occidentalists have to suffer for the boon of good roads, thus more evenly balancing their conditions with that of the macadam-and-tramway-cursed North, South, and East Metropolitans.'

Later pages of the same magazine record angrily, the law cases during the month:

'The police in the Kensington and Hammersmith districts have made sundry raids, by the aid of mounted patrols, on the bicyclists and tricyclists frequenting the wood paving in the high road. All the men were fined for furious riding, on the most absurd evidence as to their pace—14 miles an hour on a tricycle and such like nonsense! The only difference was that those who came up on Paget's days had to pay 40s. and 2s. costs, and those who were "pulled" when Sheil was sitting had only 10s. and 2s. costs to pay. But both beaks were equally deaf to the riders' assertions of innocence, and equally ready to receive as gospel the 14 miles an hour theory of the police.'

The Hammersmith stipendiary Mr Paget, was most certainly intensely disliked by cyclists for his habit of imposing the maximum penalty for riding furiously. In a worthy piece of satire, the December issue of the *Wheel World*, 1881, described a typical court hearing, which they said, 'was certainly not more exaggerated than the evidence of the police'.

'At the Sledgehammersmith Police Court, on the 31st November, 1881, John Smith, William Robinson, Thomas Brown, and James Jones appeared to answer summonses charging them with furiously riding bicycles the previous evening. Police constable ZYX 4002 deposed that he was on duty the previous evening, and saw the defendants riding at a rate of forty miles an hour; he walked after them and overtook them in Low Street, taking them to the station handcuffed. Cross-examined by the defendants the constable said he was quite sure that they were riding at a rate of eighty miles an hour, and he almost shook the creases out of his trousers in an effort to catch up with them; he could swear they were travelling at a speed of three hundred miles an hour. Police Constable ZYX 4003, corroborated this evidence, saying that he was in the London Dock area at the time, and distinctly saw the defendants travelling in Low Street, Sledgehammersmith, at a rate of five hundred miles an hour. For the defence, a number of independent witnesses were called. They claimed that the bicyclists were travelling at the slowest rate compatible with keeping the bicycles upright—viz., about four miles an hour. The defendants also said that it was impossible to ride a bicycle at the rate alleged, but Mr Paget interrupted, and said that that had nothing to do with the case, and that he should refuse to hear any more evidence for the defence. He was heartily sorry the law did not allow him to send the defendants to penal servitude for life; as it was, he should fine them the highest amount in his power, namely, forty shillings and costs each, or, in default, a month on the treadmill.'

That the law was still, in many cases, in favour of the horse as a mode of transport, is suggested by another case reported in 1881. A Mr Bussey, of the Hampshire House Hotel, Poplar, sued a man named Allcock, a foreman in the employ of Furze and Co., the Whitechapel brewers, for £4, for damages to self and bicycle, caused by defendant's reckless driving. Although the case appeared to be in the bicyclist's favour, and the defendant himself even had to be pursued and taken to the station before he would divulge his name, the County Court Judge said the bicyclist should have dismounted, as 'they could twist about and get off ten times whilst a gentleman was getting off his horse,' and on this view he non-suited the plaintiff. The much-hated Mr Paget must have been tireless in his persecution of the cyclist, for in 1881 his name is never out of the law reports of the cycling press. In every case, without fail, he fined them the maximum of 40s. and 2s. costs. But perhaps one of the strangest cases to come before the courts was the case of Parkyns v. Priest as reported in the *Law Journal Reports* October 1881 number. A month later the *Wheel World* summarised the case.

'Sir Thomas Parkyns had been convicted by a magistrate of the offence of improperly riding a tricycle of very ingenious construction. In the first place it was fitted with the ordinary treadles, but possessed, also, an auxiliary steam engine, which was so cleverly arranged, that neither in look nor in sound did it appear to be other than an ordinary tricycle. How it came to be discovered that Mr Parkyns had allied the powers of steam to those of muscle, when the ally was concealed in a box of two feet by nine inches, and gave no sound, we are not told; but in an incredulous age, the presence of the agency was detected. It is also a mystery why it was considered to put on a light skirmisher like this such humiliating shackles as the statute required—nothing less than the Locomotive Act of 1869 would satisfy its enemies. It was, in the first place, to be "driven or conducted" by at least three persons, one of whom was to walk sixty yards ahead with a red flag. It was not to sound its whistle or open its taps—neither of which appliances did it possess. It was not to blow off its steam, and various other precautions were to be taken to ensure the security of ordinary traffic from the terrors of the steam tricycle. In fact, the machine was so constructed as to have none of these terrors, and was capable of being pulled up within a few yards whether the steam was in use or not.

'Still, was it not a "locomotive propelled by steam or any other than animal power?' This was the inexorable definition of the Act of Parliament; and Lord Coleridge, Baron Pollock, and Mr

Justice Manisty were obliged to say so. The decision was obviously sound in point of statutory construction; but it cruelly and unnecessarily clipped the wings of many a lover of rapid motion. If a solemn procession of steam tricycles were formed as near Westminister as lawfully may be, with the man in front with his red flag, the man behind, and all in the strictest statutory fashion, probably Parliament would be unable to resist so melancholy a spectacle, and would give relief.'

It is not recorded whether that last cry from the heart was carried out or not, but the *Wheel World* continued with an account of another two cases, and, by juxtaposition, made a neat legal point. It is worth quoting the whole passage:

'The earlier of the two other cases is approached without any feeling of sympathy for the bicycle. In Taylor v. Goodwin, the bicyclist was found going down Muswell Hill at a rate of fourteen miles per hour. There were several passengers on the road, and one of them was knocked down. When the delinquent was brought before the Courts, it was contended on his behalf, that, however furiously he may have driven, he "was not driving any sort of carriage" within the meaning of the Highway Act. His counsel protested that he was not driving at all, but riding. On the other hand, the counsel for the Crown vouched some profound etymology, on his side, as to the meaning of "carriage" and "drive". In the result, Mr Justice Mellor and Mr Justice Lush decided that the present law was strong enough to deal with the reckless bicycles, and the conviction was affirmed.

'The third case—that of Williams v. Ellis—seems to have arisen from a too hasty generalisation of its predecessor. As bicycles were carriages within the Highway Act, so, it was argued, were they carriages within the Turnpike Act. It is one thing, however, to be bound to proceed cautiously on the road, and another to have to pay a tax. The Turnpike Act in question imposed a toll on "every carriage, of whatever description, and for whatever purpose, which shall be drawn, or impelled, or set in motion, by steam, or any other agency or power than being drawn by a horse". It must be confessed that a bicycle answers this definition as closely as the other two statutes; nor are we able to see the conclusiveness of Mr Justice

Lush's argument that "a wheelbarrow or a perambulator" would be liable to toll if a bicycle was. So much the worse, we should have thought, for wheelbarrows and, as for perambulators, they are outside the pale of male sympathy. There is more weight in the fact, that, while a horse and cart are by the Act charged 6d., the heading under which the bicycle was sought to be charged would impose a toll of 5s.

'If the case of the steam tricycle had come before the Court, before the Turnpike case, it would have been interesting to ask whether the steam tricycle ought to pay the toll. In fact, the one success which bicycle and tricycles have scored in the law Courts is the only one in which it is doubtful whether they ought to have succeeded. Probably their legal status has by no means yet been exhaustively defined. So far as the law has been able to classify them at present, they are carriages so as to have the guilt of furious driving laid at their door; they are not carriages if asked to pay toll at a turnpike gate, but they are as much locomotives as traction engines if they eke out their powers of endurance with steam, be it ever so little, or ever so carefully stowed away.'

Eventually, with the coming of the locomotive, all these problems were to be resolved, but not before the mockers had their fun. Cyclists were not completely socially acceptable yet. In a list entitled 'Things a Cyclist Ought to Know', compiled in 1882, the following are included: Never ride slowly through a crowded thoroughfare . . . Always yell at every person you meet . . . Never look where you are riding . . . Always get drunk before mounting your machine . . . In overtaking vehicles or foot-passengers, a cat-call is the best method of announcing your approach . . . The easiest method of dismounting is to fall off . . . Cleanliness is the root of all evil . . .! Although that is sheer leg-pulling the following was reported with a straight face in the *West Sussex Gazette* of January 1883:

'If anybody still thinks that we are not a musical people, here is an incident which ought to make him abase himself. The alarm bells on bicycles have suggested to some genius that the difference in the tones of various bells might be utilised to make octaves. This idea was acted upon, and an experiment was made the other night with complete success. A number of bicyclists rode through the City playing the chimes, "Blue Bells of Scotland", "Home, Sweet Home", "Auld Lang Syne", "Rule Britannia", "The Men of Harlech", and "God Save The Queen". This was not a bad repertoire to start with. We shall now have bicyclists bands, and if they can supersede the German musicians who haunt our thoroughfares, many people who have denounced bicycles will at least be softened.'

At this time (1880), bicycles cost anything between £6 and £20, and their average weight was about 50 lbs. Considering the wages paid to the average working man at this time, (factory worker, mill worker, etc.), putting the purchase of a bicycle out of reach of most of them, it is not surprising that cycling was still mainly a middle class pursuit. It was not until the advent of better working and pay conditions that the bicycle became the symbol of the emancipation of the working classes.

However, the ordinary bicycle, in spite of the fact that its popularity waned after 1885, still remained a status symbol right up to the late nineties of that century. But the numerous inventors and manufacturers of bicycles refused to stand still. Their fertile minds worked overtime on refinements, accessories and developments. Eventually there emerged a new machine which was to oust the grand old ordinary as top dog, and set the seal on bicycle design right up to the 1950's—the 'safety' bicycle, or the bicycle as we know it today.

5

JOHN KEMP STARLEY AND HIS DIAMOND FRAME

While the pennyfarthing was enjoying its peak of popularity, the developers were working away like ferrets on new ideas. Some inventors, in fact as early as 1869, look as if they got tantalisingly close to the modern safety, only to put their ideas on the shelf, or die before further development, etc. The date 1869 would be disputed by certain historians as the original date of the safety bicycle. However, the machine which is claimed as the progenitor is preserved in the *Conservatoire National des Arts et Metiers* in Paris. It is said to have been built for a clockmaker called Andre Guilmet by the French firm of Meyer et Cie, which was the first to fit wire spokes and rubber tyres to the boneshaker bicycle. If that is so, then this much more progressive machine appeared soon after the primitive machine. In other words, it was a decade ahead of its time—at a time when a decade was practically a lifetime at this stage in the development of the bicycle. The Guilmet machine consisted of a single backbone frame, with a long leaf saddle spring. The two wire-spoked, rubber-tyred wheels were of nearly the same size, and it was driven by a pedal-operated sprocket and chain-drive to another sprocket on the rear wheel. Why wasn't this machine developed immediately, since it offered much more sophistication and comfort than its contemporaries? The story goes that the Franco-Prussian War in 1870, and the fact that Guilmet was killed in it, caused the invention to lie neglected in Paris, in a loft, where it was found many years later. Doubt is cast on this story by some who say that the rear chain-drive, rubber tyres etc. could have been added later.

Another claim to the title of progenitor could be made for a design by a F. W. Shearing, details of which appeared in the *English Mechanic* of July, 1869. Unfortunately it was neither patented nor built, but at least it can claim to be one of the true forerunners. Probably the most authentic claimant is the model designed and built by H. J. Lawson in 1873/74. This machine had two medium-sized wheels of equal diameter, the rear wheel driven by a chain and sprockets. It was actually ridden on the roads of Brighton around the time of its invention.

Other attempts to get away from the heavy pennyfarthing style, even as it was gaining popular acceptance, are worth recording. In 1877 Rosseau, of Marseilles, built a bicycle which used chain drive to the front wheel. In the same year, Thomas Shergold of Gloucester produced a rear chain-drive bicycle which embodied some of the principles of the safety.

Then in 1879 Lawson came out with his third safety design, which he called the 'Bicyclette', a word used by the French for the safety style bicycle. The Bicyclette was the commercialised form of his original machines, and was an important step in the evolution of the modern bicycle. The frame was more of the cross-frame type rather than the later diamond frame, since the single-member backbone had a vertical forked support which held the pedal-spindle and chain sprocket. Steering was by handlebars which were set back near the saddle and connected to the steering head by means of a coupling rod.

The front wheel was larger than the back. Lawson apparently did not realise the importance of the design, nor the progress he had made, because he did not immediately put it into production. Years later, in 1884, he approached the BSA Company, which four years before had begun to manufacture bicycles and tricycles of their own design. He wanted them to manufacture his own design. They declined the offer, but made two prototypes for him.

At the same time, the BSA Company designed and made a safety bicycle of their own, using their standard tricycle parts wherever possible. The 32-inch rear wheel was chain-driven and the 20-inch front wheel was steered by means of a handlebar and two coupling rods. The year 1884 saw numerous designs for safeties, doubtless inspired by the Lawson originals. For instance, the Humber safety was one of the first to break away from the general form of a single main backbone frame, which had come all the way from the old boneshaker. The stiffer and more compact diamond frame in a primitive form and without a central seat pillar tube was now being used.

It is probably of value to digress at this point, on the subject of the chain drive. Right through the development of the bicycle, inventors and designers got tantalisingly close to the idea of using this type of drive for the front or rear wheel. After 1885, of course, it was in general use. But is it possible that Leonardo da Vinci hit upon the idea almost four centuries before? This question is prompted by an amazing discovery in 1965 in the National Library of Madrid. Dr Jules Piccus, of the University of Massachusetts, was looking through some old books in the Library. He noticed a gap in the card sequence of the catalogue, and asked for the corresponding volumes. Apparently the two books looked like ordinary volumes, bound in red leather with gold stampings and designs. However, when he opened them he jumped, for he recognised their importance immediately. They were lost manuscripts of Leonardo da Vinci. Dr Piccus hurriedly leafed through the books. In the first volume he found drawings on mechanical engineering, architecture and aviation. It included such brilliantly prophetic contraptions as bombs, a mill for grinding and sifting flour, and chain drives such as are today used on bicycles! Who knows, but that if da Vinci had lived long enough, he might not only have invented the bicycle, but the motor car as well.

But back to the narrative, and in 1885, the famous safety bicycle by John Kemp Starley appeared, and established the form commercially. His first design, in 1884 had a 36-inch front wheel, coupling rod steering, and a single backbone type of frame. His second design was an improved version of this. But at the suggestion of Stephen Golder, a Coventry pressman and competition cyclist, he had added direct steering and a raked head, and an adjustable saddle position, which was soon modified to the adjustable saddle pin in use today. This machine was used by Golder in a historic 100 miles race in 1885, proving its superiority over the ordinary bicycle. But the third design, the famous one, was developed from these two forerunners, and became the model for all safety bicycles until only a few years ago. The steering was direct, the head was raked, but the forks had no set to align steering-head line with the point of tyre contact with the road. The frame was in no sense triangulated. The diamond frame had really arrived. Starley's model weighed 37 lb.

However, there still remained the problem of bumping on the road, for the pneumatic tyre was yet to come. So all sorts of strange inventions were produced during this period to help absorb the road shocks. One of these appeared in 1885, made by Lindley and Biggs. The machine used a very practical spring frame. The saddle, handlebars, and pedals were all attached to a rigid triangle which was isolated from the main frame by a strong coil spring and a moveable shackle in the steering mechanism. It was popular for a few years, but was done to death by the the *début* of the pneumatic tyre, solid or hollow rubber tyres having been used up to that time.

Due to the development of the safety, a cycling boom occurred in the middle of the 1880's. For now, the bicycle, due to mass production methods, was cheaper, besides which the working class were slowly improving their lot. Cycling now cut right across the class strata. Not, however, that the upper classes were to be seen riding arm-in-arm with the horny-handed toilers—egalitarianism had not developed that far. But at least the ownership of a bicycle was no longer a status symbol of the middle classes. The new demand for bicycles could not be met by the manufacturers, so the financiers and the speculators moved in. Several cases of over-capitalisation happened, and a few years later caused a severe slump. Two or three lean years followed, also aggravated by the advent of the motorcycle and car.

But the diamond frame safety went from strength to strength. In fact, Starley's model of 1885, called the Rover, later gave that name to a famous motor car which is still in production today. The year 1890 saw the production of the Humber—the first modern form of diamond frame. This machine had all the features which are still extant today—a true diamond frame, ball-bearing raked and set steering head and fork, a spring saddle on an adjustable saddle tube, chain drive to the rear wheel, moveable rear wheel in slotted fork ends allowing chain tension adjustment, and wheels the same diameter. This particular model is of special interest as it was constructed for a journey of some 15,000 miles across Europe, America and Asia during the period 1890-1903, a trip which was successfully completed in spite of some breakages of the frame. This model is still on show at the Science Museum in London, and the frame still has the makeshift binding of telegraph wire with which it completed the last 1500 miles of the journey.

Of course journeys of tremendous length on bicycles were not uncommon around the 1880's, and became extremely popular at the turn of the century. Round about the teens of the present century, there were written a spate of books about such journeys. Books such as *Over The Alps On a Bicycle*, *Over The Pyrenees On a Bicycle*, *Bonn to Metz on Boneshakers*, *Land's End to John O'Groats On a Tricycle*, *Across Siberia On a Bicycle*, and *Through a Continent On Wheels* were common enough, and give some evidence of the hardiness of the late Victorians and Edwardians. One wonders what would happen to someone who undertook today what W. J. Reid recorded in his book, *London to Pekin Awheel*. The tradition dies hard. As late as 1964 a young Irish woman, Dervla Murphy, described in her book, *Full Tilt*, a journey from Ireland to India with a bicycle called Roz undertaken the year before. In her list of incidentals for the journey she has noted one ·25 automatic pistol and four rounds of ammunition!

Although the diamond frame safety was now in full swing, one or two other experimental types of bicycles are worth noting. Probably the most famous and most beautiful of the esoteric bicycles was the one designed by Mikale Pedersen, a Danish inventor who lived and worked in England, and who as well as being a bee-keeper, also invented the Alexandra cream spectator! The Pedersen bicycle is probably the first bicycle in history which was designed round the saddle, the saddle having been designed first! After many attempts Pedersen ended up with a seat made of silk-covered cords of different degrees of tension, running from a point in front to a cross-bar, thus forming a triangular seat. This seat he tried to fit to a conventional bicycle frame. It proved a flop—so Pedersen dispensed with the usual frame and designed one from scratch. To obtain the maximum amount of lateral rigidity, he designed it in a series of triangles, each triangle so arranged that the stresses were absorbed at its apex. The various small-diameter tubes give the whole frame structure an extra torsional stiffness, and all joints are brazed to increase frame rigidity. The long steering head and front forks form a kind of girder and turn about two widely-spaced pivots. The result is that all tubular members in the frame are subjected only to compression stress. The frame weighs only 14 lb. The hammock-type saddle is suspended from two apices of the triangular frame, and its tension may be varied to suit the individual rider. It is regarded as one of the most beautiful and luxurious bicycles ever made. It is said that Pedersen was so thorough that he kept in his bedroom, several machine tools he had designed to help in the manufacture of awkward parts for his inventions.

In 1896, Pedersen persuaded R. A. Lister, of Dursley, Glos., to manufacture them in quantity. It became known as the Dursley-Pedersen, and was claimed by the manufacturers to be 'the only perfect bicycle in existence'—a claim which is still upheld by enthusiasts today. The frame was strong enough to support six or seven men balanced on a plank. Lister stopped making them during the 1914-18 War. But a Londoner called Stephenson set up a firm called Stephenson Cantilever Cycle Company, and built and repaired machines for a little time after that. He eventually went out of business and the Dursley-Pedersen is now obsolete. An enthusiast who owns one today, in 1956 took it to a cycle repairer to have the rusty rear spokes replaced. The respoking of the rear wheel of a Pedersen is an expert's job—twelve different lengths of spoke are required. The expert kept it for a week and then returned it with the original spokes, saying, 'I've cleaned them up and trued them —those spokes are still better than any I've got in my shop'.

Following close on the heels of the diamond frame, the next big innovation was the pneumatic tyre, which not only radically changed cycling, but nearly all wheeled road vehicles. The pneumatic tyre was first patented in 1845 by R. W. Thomson, intended to make coach and carriage travel more comfortable. The idea, however, was not adopted and it was eventually forgotten. Solid and cushion rubber tyres were used to improve insulation from road shock and, later, steel rims with springs were tried out, without much success.

Then came the big break-through. In 1888, J. B. Dunlop patented a pneumatic tyre for cycles, and in the following year he was granted a patent for a pneumatic tyre consisting of an inner rubber tube and an outer cover or tread. The cover was attached to the rim of the wheel by cementing and binding. Dunlop was a Scottish veterinary surgeon who lived in Belfast, and it was in that city that the advantages of the pneumatic tyre were most dramatically demonstrated. At a race in Belfast on May 18, 1889, W. Hume, of Belfast Cruisers Cycling Club, mounted on a bicycle, the only one in the race with pneumatic tyres, won every race. He repeated the feat in Liverpool in July of that year, winning every race at the Liverpool Police Sports. Pneumatic tyres were suddenly in fashion. Other forms of pneumatic appeared, including the detachable type, the most successful being those invented by C. K. Welch who made the wired-on type, and the beaded-edge type by W. E. Bartlett. All these inventions, fostered by the Dunlop Rubber Company Ltd., soon produced the ideal tyre for bicycles and, if it comes to that, for practically every other type of wheeled vehicle. The French were also busy. The brothers Andre and Edouard Michelin took out patents in 1892 for tyres having beaded edges which were secured in position on the wheel rims by means of rings. Dunlop and Michelin, are, of course, leading names in the tyre and rubber industry to this day.

The bicycle had more or less crystallised into the form it was to have for about half a century, by the 1900's. Cycling as a week-end relaxation as well as a competitive sport, had established itself. In fact, the bicycle was looked upon by some philosophers as a truly democratic instrument. Some even saw them as an instrument for socialism. Georges Sorel, the French retired engineer and ideologue of syndicalism, who advocated violent strikes and the development of the trade unions to replace the political state, wrote in 1903:

'Dorienne gymnastics were never anything but preparation of the young for acts of war: in cities where war occupied the whole life of free men; in the days when the nobility passed most of their time on horseback. Equitation was the first of the sporting arts. But now that the bicycle provides so useful a method of transport for the working class, one must attach to the popular aesthetic the road races to which the young workers devote themselves with so much ardour.'

Here he is arguing that the aesthetic sentiments should be attached not to the productions of artists—who, he thought would disappear in the Socialist future—but to the heroic life of the productive classes. He clearly approves of the socialist bicycle. George Bernard Shaw also approved of the bicycle but more for health reasons, one feels. He saw it more as a good means of exercise, a panacea for physical rather than social ills.

Odd innovations were tried out after the general adaptation of the diamond frame as standard, but the fire of invention had died. The innovators and designers were turning their attention to the new motor cars and motorcycles in the teens of the twentieth century. In spite of the great peaks in cycling between the 1890's and the 1920's, or perhaps because of them, plus the increasing attractiveness of the motor car, the bicycle began to lose its glamour. Despite the gallant championship of men like H. G. Wells and Bernard Shaw in the 30's, the bicycle was losing ground. The increasing affluence of the 1950's dealt a severe blow. Sales of bicycles dropped by half between 1950 and 1960 in the UK alone.

This decline was only arrested by the invention of the mini bicycle, the brainchild of Alex Moulton—arrested, but not reversed. The mini, with its small wheels and rubber suspension, is recognised as the greatest revolution in bicycle design since the diamond frame.

The story of the Moulton is an interesting one. Around about 1958 or so, Mr Moulton approached Raleigh Industries —the world's biggest bicycle manufacturer—with his revolutionary ideas. Raleigh rejected the idea. Moulton went ahead and made the bicycles himself. His designs practically revitalised the industry in Britain single-handed—the Moulton became fashionable and glamorous, and won awards all over the place. But unfortunately the Moulton concern operated at a loss from 1965 to 1967. The story, however, has a happy ending. In August 1967, Raleigh Industries bought over the small-wheeled Moulton concern and retained Mr Moulton as technical adviser, Raleigh admitting that they had been wrong to reject the design in the first place

The bicycle got another much-needed shot in the arm in 1966 from Mr D. G. Wilson, a British engineer who is an associate professor of mechanical engineering at the Massachusetts Institute of Technology. He privately offered a prize of £500 for improvements in man-powered land transport design —'for the most useful and practical new contribution to the design of such a machine'. In his briefing to competitors he had this to say:

'Man-power land transport, which at the present time is confined almost entirely to that provided by the bicycle, has taken on new social significance in this automobile age. In affluent countries, the bicycle has been for many years a means of obtaining needed exercise in a pleasant and useful manner, while for others it has enabled traffic-choked streets to be navigated more rapidly than by any other method. In most developing countries the bicycle is virtually the sole means of transport (both medium- and long-distance) available to a large proportion of the population. Despite this widespread use, bicycle development has been almost at a standstill during the whole of this century. The situation is in contrast to the ferment portrayed by the bicycling handbooks of the 1880's and 90's, when almost all the details of modern designs evolved. It is the view of Mr Alex Moulton, himself responsible for the only fresh approach to bicycle design in recent years, that the motor-car siphoned off the best brains from bicycle development.

'The machine which has been evolved for the everyday rider, is despite this period of stagnated design, far from an optimum. It absorbs too much effort to propel it, chiefly because of too much aerodynamic drag. It liberally deposits oil and dirt on its rider, especially in wet weather. The most popular form of brake, the rim brake, suffers a drastic drop in efficiency in wet weather. The bicycle's reliability is poor by any standard, and repairs and maintenance take an inordinate amount of time and skill. In a collision with another vehicle or even in a fall, there is a high probability of injury to the rider. Yet despite these shortcomings and the lack of any significant research, development or design effort by any of the large, traditional bicycle manufacturers, the ordinary roadster is far from cheap. Pound per pound its cost is about three times that of a typical light car.'

As the magazine *Engineering* said about the above, it has 'an operational-research ring about it'. It certainly has! One could argue that the briefing completely ignores the magic which the traditional bicycle inspires in poets, novelists and playwrights—but that just might resurrect the Two Cultures debate, which is a mite too hefty a subject for this book. However, Mr Wilson has some worthwhile comments to make about the envisaged manually-propelled machine:

'The prize is being offered for a complete vehicle or system, not for ideas, gimmicks or research only. We leave the limits of the problem to be set by each individual or group entering. We are sure that many people will be interested in improved versions of the racing or touring bicycle, and we shall welcome their efforts. However, we feel that we have already mentioned two problems more important to our society—those of transport in the developing countries, and of transport in the big Western cities.

'In the developing countries the bicycle is the first and the most desired of the Western consumer goods. It contributes to raising the standard of living by providing mobility for people and produce. It has these major disadvantages:

'1. A bicycle is a very expensive investment, of the order of a year's income to many of the people who most need it.

'2. Bicycles, being made of materials such as ball bearings, steel tubes and pneumatic tyres, have to be imported into countries which above all things need to stimulate their own small industry.

'3. Although large and unwieldy loads are often carried in uncomfortable and unsafe conditions, the bicycles sold in most developing countries are poorly equipped for load-carrying.

'4. Existing bicycles are rather unsuited for rutted tracks of hard-baked earth, mud or sand, which are the conditions of a large proportion of the roads in these countries. An acceptable design solution for developing countries would therefore be a vehicle which uses the maximum of indigenous materials, can be constructed and maintained with local skills, and can carry goods on the vehicle rather than on the rider's head or the handlebars as is now usually the case. Obviously some qualities have to be sacrificed to reach an optimum, and it is the way the designer juggles the various competing demands, as well as his ingenuity and skill, which governs the value of his solution.

'A very different problem is found in the cities of the West, rapidly becoming clogged with traffic. It seems unlikely that the lessons of Los Angeles will soon be taken to heart so that the provision of more and more facilities for motor vehicles will no longer be considered to offer a solution to the problem. Advanced planners are, however, considering various automated-transportation schemes, from mass transit, very much as we know it today, to arrangement where people drive their own vehicles, probably battery-powered, on to various types of powered "guideways". That people should move about under their own power is, apparently, not being considered; *even walking quite short distances, will, in many cases, be quite impossible. Before long it will be realised that man has a physical and psychological need to use his muscles.* (The reader, at this point, may remember guffawing at the American journalist of almost one hundred years ago and quoted earlier in the book, who, on looking at the cycling craze, said "Walking is on it's last legs!".)

' "But even without this consideration", continues Wilson's briefing, "it is likely that some form of man-powered transport would be found to have an important place in any urban-transportation system from the economic-engineering point of view. We hope that some entries to this competition will point to interesting possibilities of solution.".'

It is significant that someone has to offer a prize in the hope of discovering another Starley, Michaux or Moulton. One wonders what new innovations will transpire from the competition. But one knows that the bicycle has already carved for itself a small but nonetheless important place in the history of mankind.

No more fitting piece could close this chapter than that written by an American journalist in 1871 in praise of the bicycle:

'When we have nationalised the stranger (the bicycle), do not let us forget his origin, but where many smooth roads meet, erect to the memory, and in honour of the inventor, a brave monument like that which surmounts the grave of him who first gave us pickles, and taught the world how to cure and barrel the bony herring.

'Let it not be said that the maker of the first bicycle went unrewarded by the descendants of that posterity who forgot Ctesibius the first organ builder, or him who introduced the grid-iron, nor yet those other anonymous benefactors to whom we owe the benefits and blessings derived from the use of door-knobs and buttons.'

6

QUEER MACHINES

'The rims were of polished mahogany while the spokes and lamp were heavily gold plated.'

The above description is of a bicycle which was exhibited at the Crystal Palace Show of 1896. One could probably write a whole book about the need of some human beings to adorn the bare bones of human inventiveness and ingenuity with the trappings of wealth—the need to build fortresses of baubles against the invasion of simplicity, and therefore truth. Such jewellery sits uneasily on the bicycle—it is much better suited to the motor-car. There is, however, no denying the rare hybrids produced from time to time by those whose curiosity was not satisfied by the mainstream bicycle of their time, or who had more money than they knew what to do with.

Some of these early experiments actually anticipated later in ventions. The following steam velocipede of the 1870's probably paved the way for the later motor cycle:

'The engine is a direct action compound engine of two cylinders, each cylinder 2½ inches diameter, 5 inch stroke. Steering gear consists of an endless chain over a grooved wheel on the engine shaft, and passing over a corresponding wheel, fixed between the forked shaft just over the front wheel. The fire box and tubes are copper, pressure 200 lbs.; but 25 lbs. of steam will be equal to a velocipede propelled by the feet'.

This, of course, was before the advent of the internal combustion engine as a workable invention. In the early 1860's there were even in existence ice velocipedes and marine velocipedes. The ice machines had a rear wheel, but in place of the front wheel was placed a ski-type platform, the idea being that this was also the steering mechanism. In 1896, Leahan's Ice Velocipede copied this idea but refined it. It had two skates and a spiked back wheel hitched up out of the way for coasting down hills, etc.

But it was the big cycling boom of the 1880's and 1890's which produced the most weird hybrids. In 1892, an amphibious velocipede rode down the Prado Avenue in Marseilles at ten miles per hour and then continued straight on into the Mediterranean. It kept going in the sea at 2¼ miles per hour on hollow double-disc wheels with rubber tyres and copper paddles. It was also fitted with a brake lever, and back pedalling put it in reverse. An even more adventurous use of the bicycle for sea was described in 1895. Invented by a Dom Ramon Barea of Madrid, it was built as follows:

'Steel cases or floats were connected by cross-bars. In the space between these is a bicycle with pedals and chain etc. The vessel is steered by a small rudder at the stern and the speed is 6 miles per hour.'

The description continued to say that it was 'well spoken of in Paris'. Another great oddity which appeared in Coney Island in the 1890's was the mobile barber's shop. This consisted of a barber's chair mounted on a tricycle which the barber rode about looking for custom.

But perhaps the most outrageous American oddity was the giant tricycle built by the Waltham Manufacturing Company in 1896. This machine had an overall length of 17 feet; the rear wheels were each 11 feet high and the front wheel was 6 feet high. It took nine men to drive the thing, each with his own chain and pedal system—four to each rear wheel and one steering. It was fitted with huge balloon pneumatic tyres and was, of course, a gimmick. It was used only for political parades, torchlight processions, and such like. It could not be used in normal traffic since it took up most of the road.

Again in 1896 the Eiffel Tower bicycle appeared. As its name implies, it was an extremely tall machine—the single bicycle was 10 feet high and the tandem model was 20 feet. Needless to say, this too, was a gimmick, and eventually became a circus accessory which is still in use today.

The ingenuity of these people in finding new and bizarre uses for the bicycle, or tricycle, seems inexhaustible. In 1895, the following description of an advertising tricycle appeared in a French publication:

'The machine represented herewith opens up a new horizon in the vast domain of advertising, in which it seemed impossible to realise still another innovation.

'As may be seen, it consists of a tricycle whose hind wheels, with very wide rims, are covered with a rubber tyre that carries, in relief, the advertisements that are desired to be made known. It will be seen at once that such ads must be quite short (founded on two or three words, for example), so that the letters may be given as large dimensions as is compatible with the width of the wheels.

'Above the wheels are placed two inking rollers, A and B, which communicate with the reservoirs R and R through tubes C and C.

'Through the intermedium of a small pulley L, and a cord b, the axle of the pedals actuates a small blower, fixed upon a shaft supported by the frame of the reservoirs. The blower sends air into the tubes which drive the dust from in front of the motive wheels. The system of tubes supporting the inking rollers is controlled by a cord attached to the extremity of the lever which the cyclist can cause to tilt in such a way as to establish contact beween the rollers.

Above, The Rover bicycle of 1885, made by James Starley's nephew, John Kemp Starley, it was the forerunner of the Rover motor-car. It was also the first diamond frame bicycle. (See Chapter 5). *Below,* The Dursley-Pedersen bicycle of 1902. A rather unique machine, built on scientific lines. (See Chapter 6)

A bicycle built for fourteen. (See Chapter 6)

The reservoirs are supported by the rear axle. The other parts of the machine do not differ from those that exist in the ordinary tricycle.'

There are no details available of the advertising campaigns carried out by this particular machine, but one would like to have heard Marshall McLuhan's verdict on the whole thing!

Perhaps the most ironical innovation was the bicycle skate, invented in 1901 by Mr Paul Jassman of Brooklyn, New York. It consisted of a double platform, with two hefty springs vertically between. The whole platform was slung between two spoked wheels. As the foot pumped up and down on the platform, the action activated a chain which drove the rear wheel. How long it survived no one knows, but it is a beautiful case of history not only repeating itself but having a good laugh at itself on the way, since the early velocipedes were reputed to have been partly inspired by childrens' skates.

Some people might regard tandems as a bit of a freak, but others could not rest happy until they had mounted three, four, five and more people on a bicycle. In 1896 the American Orient Cycle Company made a bicycle built for ten! The decemtuple has been repeated by other people as a gimmick, but surely the ultimate was reached in June 1967 by the quatrodecimalopede—the bicycle built for fourteen. The machine, thirty feet long was built by a group of fourteen young men in three months and was ridden for a distance of two miles in public from Coundon, Warwickshire, to Coventry, appropriately.

These are freaks of structural design rather than of ornamentation. But for sheer ostentation it is hard to beat the machines described by W. A. Bush in the Autumn issue of the *Boneshaker*, 1957:

'During the latter years of the Bicycle Boom, nobility vied with each other as to who could be seen on the most highly ornate bicycle. One of these was made for Lillian Russell, a leading American operatic star of the time. Every piece of metal used on the machine was heavily plated with three layers of gold and the owner's monogram was emblazoned on every one of the gold parts. The lamp was also heavily plated with gold and supplied with electric light from a tiny storage battery. This machine was valued at £500.

'At the Crystal Palace Show of 1896 an even more costly and elaborate machine than the above was exhibited. The head tube was decorated by an enormous amethyst which was encircled by a large row of pearls whilst the handlebar tips were embellished with similar precious stones. The rims were of polished mahogany while the spokes and lamp were heavily gold-plated.

'The machine was made by an American firm and was offered by them to the amateur who rode a certain distance on one of the machines in the shortest time—the amateur rules were somewhat flexible in those days.

'Another cycle exhibited at the Chicago Show was built for an American millionaire. The name plate was set in diamonds and every lug was covered in gold artistically inlaid with precious stones. On the top tube in gold was a race scene showing the finish opposite the grandstand, while the other tubes had pictures of boat races and hunting scenes on them. All of the pictures were embossed in gold and embellished with rubies, diamonds and pearls.

'The most expensive machine on record was a tandem valued at £2,000. An American machine, it was inlaid with diamonds and gold. The top tube had a baseball game engraved in gold; the other frame tubes being engraved with similar sports scenes.

'In the Smithsonian Institute in the USA is a lady's bicycle, the gift of Colonel N. J. Wiley and formerly the property of Mrs N. Wiley, the Colonel's mother. The frame is nickel-plated, with gold-plated decorations. On the steering head appear the initials M. N. W. in gold, emblazoned with small cut diamonds and emeralds. The handlebars are tipped with ivory grips, bordered with wide silver bands. The bars are embellished with gold-plated, flower-like decorations, as in the frame.'

7

THE PIONEERS

We have seen the key names put their stamp on the story of the bicycle—all of them pioneers: de Sivrac, Niepce, von Drais, Macmillan, Michaux, Lallement, Starley, Hillman, Rudge, Pedersen, Moulton. Each of them added something to the development of this unique machine, but all were engineers, inventors and innovators in the other fields as well. Pedersen was the inventor of the Alexandra cream separator and was a beekeeper, Macmillan was a blacksmith, and Alex Moulton was an engineer with the BMC motor company. This breadth of interest is in the grand tradition of Leonardo da Vinci. Another illustration of this tradition is given in a letter to the editor of the *Boneshaker* from Alfred W. Boothroyd, son of Isaac Watts Boothroyd, manufacturer of the Facile ordinary bicycle, front wheel, lever action drive:

'. . . He then bought another little ranch in the foothills of the Rockies, five thousand feet above the sea. He "batched" there alone for some time, consoling himself with poetry and memorising very much of Shakespeare, Tennyson and many other poets, in place of company.

'He married my mother there, and there I was born. However, he wearied of life and was not too fond of the American way of life, and when I was one year old, came to London and bought the firm of Ellis and Company, of Hart Street, Bloomsbury, which included the Facile bicycle, a patent rotary knife cleaner, and also the Patent Turkish Bath, which sold well, and, I believe, is still sold.

'As to the steering of the Facile, it was beautiful for riding without hands—far easier than a modern bike. As boys, we constantly rode down hills standing or kneeling on the saddle without hands.'

But perhaps the multiple interests of the cycle pioneers can best be summed up by briefly outlining the life of an archtype inventor, the man who became known as the 'Father of the Cycle Industry'—James Starley.

When still in his teens, James Starley ran away from home, his parents' farm in Sussex, in 1846, leaving the cryptic note, 'Dear Ma, sorry can't stand any more going to London, don't worry will write soon Jim.'

The main reason for his hasty departure was the complete lack of enthusiasm for his bright ideas among his immediate family circle. His father, Daniel Starley, was more interested in getting James to work on the small farm in the traditional manner than in listening to his son's bright ideas for improving the ancient plough which was a family heirloom. This, and a total disregard for his other inventions, such as a rat trap made from old umbrella ribs etc., was the final straw. So off to London he went.

He did not, however, reach London. Arriving in Lewisham, he got a job as a gardener, then moved on to the estate of John Penn, the famous engineer, as an under-gardener. When working for Penn, James invented various contraptions, including a duck-balance for the protection of ducks from water rats, a self-locking perambulator named the 'Starley Patent Self-Rocking Basinette', and he made himself a bit of pocket-money on the side by mending watches and clocks for friends. He was developing a reputation for being quite an astute mechanical engineer.

Chance now played a part in his career. When Starley was thirty-one, John Penn bought one of the new sewing-machines for his wife—an expensive present. At that time, James Starley's wife, Jane, worked as a sewing maid for the Penn household. One day the complicated machine went wrong, continuously breaking needles. Someone suggested that James be asked to have a look at it, so he was called, and took the sewing machine to his workshop. Realising that it was the most complicated piece of machinery he had ever worked on, he spent the whole evening studying the movements of all the working parts. He was frank with Penn about its complexity and suggested that it be sent back to the makers. But Penn gave him the go-ahead to attempt a repair. James stripped the machine to its last screw, examining everything as he went, and making sketches of the important parts. Eventually he found the source of the trouble, a screw which had worked loose, and assembled the whole machine again. This time it worked perfectly. Penn was very impressed, and considered that James ought to be encouraged. The fact that James had suggested modifications and improvements to the machine had added to the regard which Penn had for his young under-gardener. Penn happened to be on friendly terms with Josiah Turner, a partner in the London firm of Newton, Wilson & Co, who were the makers of the sewing-machine, and privately resolved to have a word with Turner about Starley.

Turner was impressed enough by the story of the loose screw to give James Starley a job as a mechanic in his Holborn, London, factory. Not long after, James invented his own sewing-machine which was so much of an improvement on the previous models that Turner advised him to protect the idea by Letters Patent, Turner himself putting up the necessary fees. Nor did it stop there. Josiah Turner was so convinced of the commercial potential of the new machine that he suggested they both sever connections with the Holborn factory and set up on their own. Again, it was Turner who suggested that they move to Coventry, a town badly in need of a new industry since the failure of the ribbon industry. So the move to Coventry was made in 1861, Turner providing the business dynamic and the the spur to Starley's ambitions. Turner must have been quite a magnetic character, for from the London factory he took to Coventry a number of skilled men who later became famous in their own right—men such as Singer, Bayliss, Herbert and Hillman.

The new firm was launched as the Coventry Sewing Machine Company at King Street, in the Cheylesmore district. There they produced sewing machines with fanciful but, no doubt, appropriate names such as 'The European', 'Godiva', 'Express' and 'Swiftsure'. The firm, by all accounts, prospered up to about 1867-68, moving into larger premises.

Then in 1868, Josiah's nephew, Rowley Turner burst upon the scene with the French boneshaker, and started the whole turn of events in the story of the Coventry Sewing Machine Company which has been described in an earlier chapter.

Shortly after this, Starley, in association with William Hillman, broke away from the Coventry Machine Company, to market his pennyfarthing, the 'Ariel'.

Around about the mid-1870's Starley turned his attention to tricycles, which were now becoming fashionable. In 1876 he took out a patent for the Coventry Lever Tricycle, perhaps one of the most famous of this type of machine, being particularly popular with females, because of the lack of the stability problem which afflicted the pennyfarthing. He then built a tandem version of which the riders sat back to back, but it turned out to be a little unsafe. His next move was to add a fourth wheel to the machine, making it wide enough for two riders to sit side-by-side. Various improvements led to

James then removing one of the small rear wheels, making the machine into a front-wheel steering tricycle, which had a certain amount of popularity. (This sort of circuitousness is typical of the story of the bicycle.) At this time, Starley also pioneered a machine which has been given some thought in a different form today—the folding tricycle. Called the 'Compressus' for obvious reasons, it could be folded to take up minimum space when not in use, or for packing into a train or cart. (Today's folding mini-motorbikes can be packed into the boot of a car, and are used by some enterprising souls for travel in traffic-congested cities.)

As pointed out in a previous chapter, James Starley invented the tangent spoke wheel (still used in today's bicycles). When it was first introduced it caused some controversy—rival manufacturers looked askance at paying royalties for using it, and some even suggested that it was mechanically unsound. Starley made a practical reply to these criticisms—he set about constructing a giant tangent-spoke wheel, and incorporated it into a huge pennyfarthing. It was kept under cover until the opening day of a cycle show at Leamington Spa. There was quite a stir when it was finally unveiled and ridden about the show by Starley's two sons, especially as the front wheel was seven feet in diameter. The trouble was that, because of the size, the rider had difficulty reaching the pedals when they were down, a problem which was solved by fixing the machine with a lever gear arrangement with treadles. The demonstration effectively squashed any further criticism of the tangent-spoke wheel.

But one of James Starley's most startling inventions was the differential gear—startling not only in the manner of its discovery, but also in its implications for the future of the motor-car industry. James and his son William went riding one afternoon on a four-wheeled machine which had been made by coupling two pennyfarthings together side-by-side, and a long connecting rod joining the two large wheels. Two saddles were fixed above this. Apparently this hybrid was promptly christened 'Starley's Wonder' and, later, 'Honeymoon Sociable'.

They were planning to go to Birmingham and back—a nice Saturday afternoon ride. On the run, the machine acted rather oddly. It swerved going downhill, and was hard work uphill. On one particular hill, James urged William to greater effort, which William followed to the letter. He pedalled like mad and the machine suddenly swerved, forcing the wheel on James Starey's side into the ditch and throwing James off the vehicle.

After recovering, James sat down and pondered the problem of the swerving wheel. Then he hit on the solution to the whole thing, and hastily sketched it on a piece of paper. He showed it to William, excitedly explaining that the present model would not work properly except with two riders of equal strength and consistency. What was needed was a two-piece axle, cut in the middle, with bevel wheels in the middle, cut, with gear teeth, in a certain way. He explained to William that with the new arrangements, no matter how hard one or other of the riders pedalled, the wheels would go round independently. They both rushed back to the workshop where they worked till late, James carving out of wood a model of the new gearing system, William hunting out old cog wheels, etc. On the following Monday morning, James was up early and off to London to see about patenting his latest invention. This was the birth of the differential gear, with which every motor-car in the world today is equipped.

James Starley died in the Summer of 1881, but his sons and his nephew, John Kemp Starley, lived on to nourish the great tradition which he had originated. John Kemp Starley's father, James's brother John, had written in 1872 to James asking him if he could get his son a position in a factory in Coventry, as he showed some promise as an engineer. James immediately got him a job in the firm of Haynes and Jeffries, who made components for Starley's bicycles—William the youngest son, eventually took over the leadership of the firm, which expanded during the bicycle boom of the 1880's and 90's. He was almost as inventive as his father and accumulated 138 patents to his name. His inventions were on subjects as varied as venetian blinds, railway brakes, golf clubs, roller skates, tubular steel furniture and animated photography.

The next Starley to make a big splash was John Kemp. When he had started at the firm of Haynes and Jeffries, he was about twenty-two, but he had lived with his uncle James, watched, and learned a lot. After a while, John Kemp felt the urge to break out on his own, and this he did shortly after the death of James. Not having any capital he looked around for a partner and found one in William Sutton, a keen cyclist who owned a shop in Coventry. He put up the capital and John left his firm, and so the partnership of Sutton and Starley was born at the Meteor Works, in West Orchard, south of Corporation Street.

At first they made only pennyfarthings and Meteor Tricycles. However John Kemp was perpetually seeking improvements to the large wheel bicycles. Slowly the safety began to evolve —as mentioned in a previous chapter. While working on these designs, Starley kept them very secret. It is purported that he and Sutton used to take the new machines out into the country in a pony-trap and test them in secret. Eventually the first Rover prototype was made, followed quickly by the second and then the third model, which influenced so many subsequent bicycle designs. The invention a few years later of the pneumatic tyre was to consolidate the Rover's position as the leading design type. That John Kemp realised the importance of the pneumatic tyre to the bicycle is demonstrated by the following letter written to him by J. B. Dunlop in 1897:

'Everybody knows that you set the fashion in the introduction of the rear driven safety, but few know that you were the first gentleman in England to appreciate the pneumatic tyre. Long before the Pneumatic Tyre Company was floated, you sent hubs and spokes to Eldin & Co., Belfast, to have the wheels built and fitted with pneumatic tyres.

'It was my intention to take the wheels when built, over to you with a view to floatation. Edlin was in a small way and was very busy and therefore unable to complete the wheels in a reasonable time, hence the project fell through. I have pleasure in sending at your request two photos and hope to have yours in return.'

John Kemp Starley had interests as wide as his famous uncle and cousin William. Eventually he had eighty-seven patents to his name, mostly, but by no means all, concerned with bicycles and accessories. He also patented ideas for cork screws, stair-tread mats, and electric furnaces.

This particular Starley was a man who did not stand still. Even as his Rover bicycle was catching on with the public, he was thinking of the future, and of powered road machines. In 1888 he began building an experimental prototype of a power-driven tri-car in the Meteor Works. It was a small car and was to be driven by electrical power, and is believed to have been the first motor-car built in Coventry. However, when the prototype was ready for the road, the law of the land frustrated his purpose. It was an offence at that time to drive at more than four miles per hour on the roads, and even at that speed one had to be preceded by the famous 'man with the red flag'. John Kemp arrived at a typical solution. He shipped the whole motor-car across the channel to France, where such restrictions did not exist. His actual testing ground in France was Deauville, later to become famous as a racing centre. During the tests his car achieved an average of about eight miles per hour, which Starley found very satisfactory. This was, in fact, the first Rover car. He died in 1902, without the satisfaction of seeing his company develop into one of the world's leading car manufacturers, but probably happy enough to have achieved what he did.

Although John Kemp went from success to success, his cousin William, James's son, did not have such an easy ride. He was one of the victims of the great bicycle boom which eventually burst, taking with it those who had been unwise enough or greedy enough to get on the bandwagon. By 1898 Coventry was in the grip of a trade recession. The bicycle industry had over-produced to such an extent that there were not enough market outlets for the product. Very soon dozens of firms were ruined and thousands of investors lost their money. Certainly William Starley was financially ruined. But notwithstanding that, he went to London and started from scratch again, and in fact outlived his cousin John Kemp by almost quarter of a century.

Almost certainly the biggest cycle manufacturer in the world is the Raleigh Company (now known as Raleigh Industries), a part of the big combine, Tube Investments, but the beginnings of Raleigh are as small and humble as any other cycle firm so far encountered. By about the late 1880's a young Englishman, Frank Bowden, was bound for England from Hong Kong. It must have been a sad journey, for his doctors had told him: 'Go back to England. You have only a few months to live.' But Frank Bowden was only twenty-eight years old, had a small fortune in his pocket, and a strong will to live. Besides, he was not satisfied with the doctors' verdict.

On his return to England he consulted a doctor in Harrogate who told him: 'If you want to regain your health, ride a bicycle'. Sure enough, having taken his doctor's advice, six months later, he was a fit man. He was pretty impressed with the bicycle, too. So he decided to invest some of his money in bicycles. He immediately started to trace the makers of the bicycle which had returned his health, and eventually discovered a small workshop in Raleigh Street, Nottingham, owned by Messrs Woodhead and Angois, who had formed a partnership in 1887 and were producing ten bicycles a week.

After a thorough inspection of the work they were doing,

Bowden was impressed enough to suggest an injection of his capital. They agreed and a new partnership agreement was draw up giving Bowden a free hand in the running of the business. One of the first things he did was to purchase a four-storey factory on Russell Street, Nottingham, where the first Raleigh bicycles with one-inch diameter tubing were manufactured.

For the first two years Frank Bowden financed the enterprise himself, and in 1890 he floated the Raleigh Company with himself as chairman, Mr Woodhead as business manager, Mr Angois as chief designer, and Mr E. C. Farrow as company secretary. During the first three years the company made a total profit of £13,000.

About this time, G. P. Mills a civil and mechanical engineer, who later replaced Angois as chief designer and works manager, was engaged as a draughtsman at a salary of £1,000 a year—quite a salary for those times. Mills held the record for the Land's End to John O'Groats tandem race, and had actually designed a number of tandems himself. It was on one of these machines that he and the famous Bidlake won the Land's End to John O'Groats record. His next design was a cross-frame machine called the *Modele Superbe*. One of the most expensive models of this machine was made for Lady Jane Fane, of Lincolnshire. Tailor-made, it had the normal green finish but the lining was finished in 18 carat gold leaf and the headcrest and Lady Jane's initials were made of solid gold. The wheels and rims were copper plated and the spokes were green enamelled. By 1896 the firm had outgrown itself and new premises were designed by Mills and erected on Faraday Road, Lenton.

In 1902 Henry Sturmey and James Archer—a schoolmaster and an engineer, approached Frank Bowden with their new invention—the three-speed gear hub. Raleigh immediately went into production of these gears which proved to be the prototype for the great majority of this type of gear which have subsequently been produced. Raleigh expanded fast after that, riding the cycle boom with ease. In fact, Frank Bowden travelled around the world so many times, appointing agents and so forth, that he was elected a member of the Royal Geographical Society.

Some idea of the size of the Raleigh empire can be garnered from the names of the firms they have taken over during their lifetime: Rudge-Whitworth, Humber, Triumph, Sunbeam, BSA, Brooks Saddles, Phillips, Hercules and Norman and . . . Moulton.

8

THE RACERS

The tragic death of Tom Simpson during the 1967 Tour de France, connected as it was with the controversy of stimulants and making front-page news in the English papers, probably more than anything brought this fantastic and famous race to the attention of non-cycling Britons. It must be difficult for an Englishman to appreciate the passions and tensions which this race rouses in both competitors and onlookers alike. Described as the 'Greatest Show on Earth', it is probably the nearest thing to a Roman Holiday that the present-day Continent has to offer. The fact that the English have not embraced the competitive aspects of cycling with the passion of the Continentals says volumes about their character, and their general insularity. However, in September 1967, a much-publicised attempt was made to re-introduce six-day racing to England after an absence of fifteen years.

The date is ironic for almost a hundred years before on Whit Monday, 1868, the first organised bicycle race to be held in England was held near the Welsh Harp, Hendon, just a day after James Moore had won the famous bicycle race in

Paris. The following year John Mayall, a friend of Turner, made the first attempt to reach Brighton on a boneshaker, but became exhausted at Redhill and abandoned the attempt. He made another attempt soon after, in the company of two friends, and the three of them successfully completed the trip in sixteen hours. *The Times* acclaimed the feat in an article headlined, 'An Extraordinary Velocipede Feat'. But two months later, C. A. Booth, a skating champion, covered the same distance on a boneshaker in only 7½ hours. In those days a distance of 30 miles covered in an 8-hour day was considered a good average.

The first big name in racing must have been James Moore, an Englishman who lived in Paris for a time. He was the Reg Harris, Tom Simpson, Fausto Coppi, or Anquetil of his time. He rode and won the first ever recorded cycle race which was held at St Cloud, Paris, on May 31, 1868, and which was run over a distance of 1200 metres.

The first long-distance cycle road race was held on November 7, 1869, between Paris and Rouen. Apparently there were more than two hundred starters, five of whom were women. Again James Moore won the race, covering the distance of 83 miles in 10 hours, 25 minutes. Also in 1869, the *Veloce Club de Paris* was formed and a permanent cycle track was built on the Vesinet race course near Paris, and another was opened at the same time at Crystal Palace, London. As well as being a leading bicycle champion, or probably because of it, James Moore also made some improvements to the design of the bicycle as such. Incidentally, the Star ordinary bicycle, an American invention with the small wheel in the front and the big wheel at the back, was often used for racing and was particularly suited to the sport. The drive mechanism on this machine was by levers instead of cranks, a peculiarity of which was that the pedals worked independently so that, if necessary, both could be pressed down at the same time. This was a big advantage in racing for producing a spurt or a quick start.

During the 1870's, as the popularity of cycling established itself, many clubs were formed in England, France and America. Perhaps the oldest surviving cycling club in the world is the Pickwick, which was formed in 1870—to be exact on June 22nd of that year. Six enthusiasts met at the Downs Hotel, Hackney Downs, East London, to form the Pickwick Bicycle Club in memory of Charles Dickens (who was a keen cyclist) and who had died on the ninth of June that year. Club regulations included the adoption by each member of a sobriquet allotted to him by the Committee—the name of some character from the Pickwick Papers. He was traditionally addressed as such at all meetings of the club, and was forbidden to change his sobriquet without the sanction of the committee. John Kemp Starley was one of the early presidents of the club, being called Justice Starleigh from the Bardell trial. The Dungarven was started a few months later in the provinces, and soon after clubs mushroomed throughout the country. Aptly, since Cambridge is one of the last outposts of the bicycle at the present time, the largest membership during this period was claimed for the Cambridge University Club, with a total of 280. The Bicycle Touring Club formed at Harrogate in 1878, was the first touring club of its type, and boasted a membership of over 500. In 1883, the name was changed to the Cyclists Touring Club, by which it is still known to the present day.

By 1879, the mile had been covered in under 3 minutes and a hundred miles had been covered in less than 8 hours. But like any other sport, record gave way to record as better and better machines were developed and cyclists became more proficient. America, justifiably famous for its crop of negro athletes, can only boast one major negro champion cyclist. Marshall Taylor was born in 1878, and is the only negro ever to hold both the American and the World professional cycle racing championships, He was unofficial national champion in 1898, co-champ in 1899, champ in 1900, and world champ in 1899.

But perhaps the most colourful American cyclist was Charley

A pennyfarthing race in 1890. (See Chapter 8)

A 'Scorcher' in St James's Park, 1897. 'Scorcher' was one of the nicknames for the bloomer girls. (See Chapter 9)

'A halt by the way for a quiet smoke and some small repairs.' (See Chapter 9)

Murphy, who became known throughout the States as 'Mile-a-minute Murphy'. A crack amateur cyclist, Murphy boasted that he could keep up with any locomotive built, provided there was a wind-shield at the back. Everyone thought he was crazy, until Hal Fullerton, a special agent with the Long Island Railroad, got to hear about the boast. The possibility of a tremendous publicity stunt suggested itself to Fullerton. After months of preparation, Fullerton had laid a smooth wooden track over the sleepers on a 3-mile stretch of track at Maywood Station. A hood was built around one end of the passenger car to shield Murphy from the fierce slipstream. Then, on June 30, 1899, the whole thing was ready for the experiment. One mile from the starting line, the engineer opened the throttle. When they hit the starting line they were doing 60 miles per hour and Charley was still right behind the locomotive. Exactly 57 and four fifths of a second later, they crossed the finish line, a mile away. Ever since, Charley was known as 'Mile-a-minute Murphy', but his triumph must have turned sour on him, for in later years he complained that he had become the 'laughing-stock of the world'.

In 1928 at Monthlery, France, Leon Vanderstuyft, paced by a motorbike, covered 76 miles, 504 yards in one hour. Then in 1941, one of the most spectacular records was set up by Alfred Letourneur on a highway near Bakerfield, California. Letourneur, a six-day racing star, rode behind a windshield built onto the back of a motorbike driven by Romney Householder, and actually clocked up a speed of 108.92 miles per hour, covering an officially measured mile in a time of 33.05 seconds. He was riding the highest geared bicycle ever built—the front sprocket had 57 teeth, and the rear had 6 teeth.

The first six-day cycle race in the States took place in 1891 in Madison Square Garden, New York, on high-wheelers. There were 40 starters and 6 finishers, the winner being William Martin, who covered 1466 miles and 4 laps during the race. During a later six-day race in 1898, Charlie Millar, riding a pneumatic tyred safety, covered 2093 miles and 4 laps. The greatest advantages of the pneumatic tyre had already been demonstrated by Hume in Belfast when, in 1891, Charles Terront won the Paris-Brest-Paris road race of 750 miles on the then new demountable Michelin pneumatic tyre. He beat the favourite by 8 hours. 'Success', he is reported as saying, 'was due to the new tyre which took less time to change'. Two trainers rode beside him with bells, ringing them to keep him awake.

All of which, unknown to these early champions, was leading up to the birth of the most famous cycle race in the world—the *Tour de France*. On the 17th January, 1903, the newspaper *L'Auto*, which had been known as *L'Auto-Velo*, announced the annual calender of events held under its patronage. Among the events were four for cyclists, one of which was described as '. . . a great cycle race over an interesting route . . .' Two days later the details of the tour were announced in the paper, complete with a total prize figure of 20,000 francs. It was to be a six-stage race covering 1,510 miles from May 31st to July 5th. It would start and finish in Paris.

The whole thing was thought up by Henri Desgrange, himself a cyclist of no mean ability, and who was then working as a journalist for *L'Auto*. As far as publicity and interest went, the first tour seemed headed for success. Advertisers bought lots of space in *L'Auto*, and sponsors came forward. There was, however, one snag—a week before the tour was to begin, only fifteen competitors had actually entered. Desgrange acted fast and made some changes. The race was reduced to three weeks, the entry fee was reduced, expenses were guaranteed, and the race was not to be run unless a minimum of 50 competitors turned up. The reshuffle worked. There were seventy-eight entries and sixty actually turned up at the start. Twenty-one of these appeared on the finishing list.

The second tour, in 1904, was almost the last as well. The first had, apparently, unleashed a tremendous spate of partisanship and passion, and riders in the second race were under constant attack from hostile crowds and supporters of rival riders. The first incident was an ambush after midnight outside St Etienne. A gang of partisan spectators armed with sticks and clubs set about the riders, the plot being to allow a certain Benoit-Faure, a native of St Etienne, to reach Marseilles first. Fortunately, only one rider had to retire. However, on the final day, on the road to Paris the worst attack of the race happened. At one point the road was barricaded with felled trees, fencing and farm implements. Having got over the obstructions, the riders then found the ground strewn with broken glass and nails. Desgrange was bitter about the whole thing and announced in *L'Auto*: 'The Tour is finished, and I can assure you that the second edition has been the last—killed by its own success, by the uncontrollable passions which it has released. The fanatical spectators have cause us to forget any ideas of preserving the *Tour de France*.'

But this Tour had hit the headlines of the national papers and a lot of questions were asked. There certainly had been irregularities. Eventually it was all sorted out, and a number of riders had to forfeit their prizes. That put a stop to night riding. For a number of years, parts of the Tour were bedevilled by fanatics who put nails and glass on the roads. This eventually died out, but sabotage of a different kind continued—interference with riders' bicycles at night. In the 1910 Tour, for instance, one rider named Gustave Garrigou fell victim to a nasty piece of sabotage. He recounted the incident in 1960:

'That day we were crossing Nimes-Perpignan for the eighth stage. I took care the previous night, as always, to take my Alcyon cycle up into my room at Nimes. It might have seemed a needless precaution becaues our team had so far dominated the Tour. The only scuffling for places was between ourselves. Anyway I forgot to lock my door, a mistake which cost me dearly.

'We were going through Lunel at about 3 a.m. when my front wheel gave up—ball bearings spilling everywhere. Someone had done a good job of unfixing the hub, and I hadn't noticed a thing. So I had to find a mechanic—at 3 a.m.—then search for bearings of the right size to replace those I had lost. To be blunt I lost an hour and a half over that. And I had been within seconds of Faber (a rival) . . .'

Part of the legend of the Tour is not only the toughness of the race itself but the astonishing strength, stamina and endurance of the riders. The big names in the early part of the century were Faber, Garrigou, Petit-Breton and Georget. It would be impossible for a race of this nature not to attract some colourful characters. In the 1911 Tour there was a rich baron called Pepin, who took along two valets to act as pacemakers—and there was also Dozel, who started the Tour with a supply of photographs of himself which he distributed to the crowds along the route. Tommy Simpson also endeared himself to the spectators by his clowning.

The coveted prize of the Tour is, of course, the yellow jersey which marks the leader of the race at any particular stage and also the overall winner. It was first worn by an Englishman (but not for long) when Tommy Simpson wore it for one day in the 1962 Tour. The first Irishman to wear the symbolic jersey was Seamus Elliott, who kept it for three days during the 1963 race.

The idea of the yellow jersey was started in 1919. Apparently, during a meeting of journalists, officials and team managers as the race was proceeding, suggestions on how to improve the conduct of the race were asked for. Alphonse Bauge said that the riders would appreciate some form of distinction for the race leader as the position changed hands so often. It was often difficult to spot the leader and keep an eye on him, and also, the spectators would appreciate a means of spotting the leader as well.

Henri Desgrange asked Bauge what he suggested as a mark, and Bauge said that, since the colour of the sponsoring paper, *L'Auto* was yellow, why not let the race leader wear a yellow jersey. Desgrange was thrilled with the idea and immediately phoned Paris for a supply of the jerseys. A few days later, Eugene Christophe, the first man in the history of the Tour to wear the yellow jersey, was wearing his. Since 1947, all yellow jerseys in the Tour are embroidered with the initials H. D. in perpetuation of the name of Henri Desgrange. The green jersey is given to the rider who has taken the lead in the points clasification, which is based on the addition of points for a rider's daily placings. No one has yet won both yellow and green jerseys on a Tour.

Because of the toughness of the Tour, no disgrace attaches to the rider who finished last in the race. In fact there is even a special name for him with a certain irony about it—he is known as the 'Red Lamp'. Although some stars have been known to retire rather than become Red Lamp, aspiring stars have also been known deliberately to finish in that position for the publicity.

The ardour, sweat, sheer back-breaking work and, above all, passion which is part and parcel of the Tour has never been captured better than in the splendid film recently made by Claude Lalouche—'In Search of the Yellow Jersey'.

9

'GIVE ME YOUR ANSWER, DO'

The song, 'Daisy, Daisy,' probably one of the most famous pop songs in the world, was, contrary to popular belief, inspired by a *side-by-side* tandem bicycle, and not the more conventional type. It says something for the stamina of the song that, even today—almost seventy years after it was written—the number of people who do not know the words of the chorus could be counted on one hand. It also says something for the speed of social change in those days that only ten years before the song was written, women were still being stoned in the streets of London for riding high-wheeled machines. The general cry of derision on the lips of urchins and policemen—'Monkeys on wires'—could still be heard up to about 1890. (Rarely has a common enemy made such strange bedfellows as London street urchins and London bobbies!) The other well-known term of abuse at the time—'Cads on castors' —is much more genteel and betrays its middle-class origins.

Whether the bicycle has ever actually been used for lovemaking is not recorded, but it certainly has been used as a sort of social lubricant and has led, no doubt, to the downfall of many a young lady, in more ways than one. And it certainly was highly instrumental in the big drive for female emancipation and sexual equality.

In this respect just as symbolic as the bike are the bloomers—those beautiful female trousers which provide an ever-recurring motif in the fashion world when designers have run dry of ideas. Ever since 1850, they have been popping up at intervals of twenty-five or thirty years to inform and renourish the fashion scene. Again, contrary to popular belief, they were not named after the first woman to wear them.

In 1848, in New York, USA, there was a progressive community called the Oneida Community. During that year the men of the community were building a new meeting house, and the women wanted to help. The only snag was that standard female dress at that time consisted of a long skirt which swept the ground, worn over numerous petticoats and crippling tight-laced stays. Women could hardly breathe, never mind carry logs of timber. They took drastic action. Every adult female in the place started wearing an American version of Oriental harem dress—pantaloons, with a skirt reaching to just below the knee. But it was not until 1851 that the revolutionary dress was to be seen outside the community. It was in that year that Mrs Elizabeth Smith Miller paid a visit to her cousin, Elizabeth Cady Stanton, of Seneca Falls, New York. To say that she caused a sensation among the neighbours would be putting it mildly, for she was wearing one of the new daring trouser dresses. Sadly enough, although Mrs Miller was responsible for popularising the style outside Oneida, it does not bear her name.

At the time, Mrs Amelia Bloomer was editing a reform magazine, called *Lily*. When she heard about Mrs Miller's new dress, she went into eulogies about it, praised her for her courage and immediately followed her example. The public, and especially the press, pounced on the outlandishness of both the dress and Mrs Bloomer's name, and ever after they were known as 'Bloomers'. And in spite of Mrs Bloomer's refusal to take the credit and her protestations that Mrs Miller was the original revolutionary, the name stuck. The press and the public refused to call them 'Millers'.

The women who wore the new style were, of course, mercilessly ridiculed, caricatured, parodied and generally made fun of. But they stuck it out and the craze lasted for about eight years, before giving in to the ridicule. Ordinary skirts were back. But in the 1890's, with cycling riding a peak of popularity, bloomers came into their own again, as ideal cycling dress for women. The USA again led the field in this particular breakthrough, as it had done in 1850.

The fact that grudging assent had been given to the idea that cycling was now as much a female pastime as a male one, and the thought that at last he could now share his pleasure with his beloved, probably inspired an anonymous Victorian poet of dubious talent to pen the following immortal lines entitled, *The Passionate Cyclist And His Love*:

Come ride with me and be my love,
And I will all the pleasures prove
Of sauntering in the shady lanes,
Where golden-tinted summer reigns;
And as our wheels revolve with speed,
Fair nature's beauties we can heed;
If these to you delights will prove,
Come ride with me and be my love.

But there had been a lot of opposition to the idea of women and girls cycling. Some people went to great lengths to keep it a male preserve. Writing in 1870, one apologist for the 'male only' line had this to say:

'It would no doubt be mighty pleasant to go out velocipeding with your fair friends, each mounted on his or her own bicycle, but custom and nature revolt against it, and there can be no doubt, but that it is in the eternal "Fitness of Things" that it should be so. At least half the interest of one sex in the other arises from their respective dependent and protective positions. When a lady velocipedes she destroys all this kind of subtle interest and thereby loosens one of the sweetest and firmest bonds of existence. Every velocipedestrienne ought to be compelled to wear blue stockings.'

One supposes there will always be this type of reactionary thinking, especially where females are involved. But in the end the revolutionaries won through—in the case of bicycles, anyway. The American poet writing in 1870, and quoted below, cleverly combined a love poem with a plea for more cycling and a salute to the bicycle:

She saw him en velocipede,
A-kitting up the road,
And pitty-pat and pitt-pat,
Her little heart lit gold,
And soft she sobbered to herself,
'Though fast his paces be,
He cannot dust so quickly, but that
My heart keeps up with he.

O, *vive la belle* velocipede!
Which digs along the street,
But that which I do chiefly vive
Is he who does the feat.
I cannot help aloving him,
Nor he aloving me,
Velocipedestrination is
A thing that has to be.

When cycling became popular with women, no doubt a lot of manufacturers were torn between their prudishness and the desire to make money by getting on the bandwaggon. One man resolved it in a peculiar way, judging by the advertisement proclaiming the new machine.

His name was Sterling Elliott, an American, and also inventor of the Elliott addressing machine:

'A new departure in bicycle construction, and yet based on some of the oldest facts the world possesses. The use of hickory timber for the wheels and framework of carriages has passed the experimental stage by several thousand years; but when we began the manufacture of our hickory bicycle, the feeling toward us, as exhibited by the cycling public, was about equally divided between pity and contempt. But the Hickory Bicycle—

'Is a thing of such unique construction,
When seen more oft, familiar with its grace,
They first investigate, then purchase, then make pace.

It has been our aim to build a bicycle which man or woman could ride and still be a Christian. If we have not succeeded you can easily prove it.'

The above is probably the first example of religion being used as an inducement to buy a bicycle. However, it still took some time for women's clothes to assume common-sense proportions for cycling, in spite of the beach-heads established in the USA on this front. As has been mentioned in a previous chapter, James Starley went to the extent of designing a big-wheel ladies' bicycle to *fit around* the ridiculous and voluminous skirts of Victorian women, rather than even suggesting the rationalisation of the clothes. The bicycle, needless to say, was a failure. Prudishness was the order of the day, right into the late 1890's. Conservative women stuck to their long skirts. And just in case anyone should catch a glimpse of stocking—which in the words of the song was regarded as 'something shocking'—they also wore high-buttoned shoes or laced boots. We can be grateful for one thing at least—high-laced boots were a far cry from the mediaeval chastity belt, and probably a lot more comfortable to wear.

But just in case this did not work, someone actually invented a foot shield for ladies' bicycles. He was an American called Theron R. Cherry, from West Virginia—a locale which may be significant. The screen was like an umbrella split in two, and could be folded back past the pedals 'to protect the feet and ankles from view when mounting or riding, and to prevent skirts from being blown about the limbs'. It also provided for a front screen 'to close the space and prevent draught between the side screens'.

Writing in the Lady's Column of *Bicycling News* in the late eighties of the last century, 'Violet Lorne' had this to say on the subject:

'It cannot be too often nor too clearly understood by novices of the wheel that style of costume unlikely to attract attention or remark is the correct wear for the cyclist. Neither brilliant blazers nor obtrusive garments of any sort have a look either business-like or suggestive of good breeding which makes a woman shrink from being conspicuous, and among women of good taste they will never be popular.

This provides a startling contrast to what the fashion writers of 1967 were saying. One recently wrote:

'Bicycling fashions this year have just completed a full turn of the fashion wheel. For bloomers . . . and the old style knickerbockers are back in the wheel world.'

Another wrote:

'What happens if it rains and you've just had your hair done? . . . But (I) develop raging cold and such badly knocking knees that Bermuda shorts are out of the question. Buy trouser suit . . .'

'Violet Lorne' would have a blue fit and forty kittens, and probably disappear in a cloud of Victorian apoplexy! But perhaps she might feel vindicated by the finish of the last writer's article:

'And, unless you are prepared to chain yourself as well as the bicycle to the railings, don't believe the emancipated bit. We still need a Rational Dress League—and a skirt in the saddle bag'.

However, the problems of social intercourse for the cyclist

have been in the minds of writers ever since the days of the boneshaker. One erstwhile chronicler, writing in 1869, posed a number of questions on various matters touching the niceties of good manners:

'If a fellow goes with his velocipede to call upon a lady, whose house has no front yard, and no back yard, and there are a lot of boys in the front of it ready to pounce on his machine, and the lady is smiling through the window, what is he to do?

'If a fellow, riding his velocipede, meets a lady on a very rough bit of road, where it requires both hands to steer, is he positively required to let go with one hand to lift his hat? And if so, what will he do with his machine?

'If a fellow, riding his velocipede, overtakes a lady carrying two bundles and a parcel, what is he to do with it?

'If the hind wheel of a fellow's machine flings mud just above the saddle, ought he to call on people who do not keep a duplex mirror and a clothes brush in the front hall?'

The poor fellow's dilemma seems insoluble, but then, that was in the days when to have offered the young lady a lift on the cross-bar, would have been to have courted social ostracism, if not worse.

For a really startling assertion of the great link between the female and the bicycle, one must turn to a Mrs F. Harcourt Williamson, writing in 1897:

'It was women who first made bicycling the fashion. At least ten years before there was any idea of women ever riding on wheels, the bicycle had made its way into popular favour as a useful and hygienic means of locomotion; but it might have been always confined to the business of the comparatively few instead of being applied to the pleasure of the many, if by some happy chance it had not been taken up by the right people and straightaway become the craze of the season, while it is well-known that what once is approved by the classes, will in the end be patronised also by the masses.

'. . . and, remembering how only a few years ago the appearance of a cyclist was greeted with derisive cheers, and how mischievous urchins took delight in throwing down their caps before a machine in the hopes of an upset; remembering, too, how adventurous women were almost mobbed upon their first appearance riding—it is difficult to realise that now all the royalties in Europe (except the Emperor of Germany, who is very dogged in his disapproval of the sport suitable for ladies!) are patronising the sport; and boys in red uniforms with the name of "Gavin" on their caps, may be seen waiting on the steps of Mayfair and Belgravia Mansions to clean the aristocracy's machines.

'History has not recorded which of the fashionable women was first to discover the delight of whirling all over the country on two wheels; but it was certainly Lady Norreys who first excelled in this direction, and I can well remember seeing quite a little crowd collected at her door in Great Cumberland Place to see her start upon her ride, when, regardless of her admiring audience, she jumped lightly onto her machine, and ringing her bell smartly once or twice as warning, wheeled away, with her dogs frisking and barking behind her. She knows nothing whatever of fear; and with quite unruffled countenance will cross that dangerous wide space between Constitution Hill and Piccadilly, and turn up the hill of Hamilton Place, as unconcerned and cool as though she were on one of those beautiful broad level roads in France, where vehicles are so delightfully few and very far between. She is always very neatly dressed, generally in dark blue, with white revers on her coat and a natty sailor hat.

'Another little lady who led the way where this fashion was concerned was Lady Cairns, who, like Lady Norreys, is very small in stature and slim, while it is well known that slender figures look their best upon wheels. She is a very plucky rider too, and one hears of her in the neighbourhood of Windsor flying downhill with two or three companions as daring as herself, all hand-in-hand, and not one of them even attempting to guide their machines, but trusting entirely to balance. The very good riders all pride themselves upon being able to ride without touching their handles; and Miss Muriel Wilson, who is another smart cyclist, has been seen again and again in Hull, which is the nearest town to Tranby Croft, with one hand thrust into her coat pocket, and the other engaged in holding up her parasol.

'I have laid it down, as a rule, that only small women look their best upon wheels, but this, like every other rule, has brilliant exceptions. Few women ride more gracefully than Mrs W. H. Grenfell.

I have seen her dressed all in soft green, a tweed skirt and velvet Tam-O-Shanter looking more distinguished than any one else as she passed through the throng in Hyde Park. Lady Minto, who bicycles nearly as well as she skates, and Lady Griffin, who is also a very pretty rider, are both generally seen in navy blue and white, with sailor hats; and Lady Lurgan, one of the very best bicyclists, spent much of her time, when she had a house on the river, not on the river itself, but on wheels.

'The whole secret of a woman looking well upon her bicycle lies in the cut and the hang of her skirt. There have been numberless inventions, some of them happy ones, but the very best skirt of all, in my opinion, is one made by Busvine, the great habit-maker, fitting the figure perfectly, and cunningly stretched and shrunk (as habit-skirts are) so to do.

'I have seen black look very well on a bicycle. Mrs Arthur Paget has a wonderful skirt—made in America, I think—which is perfectly shaped like a habit and makes her look even slimmer than she is; and many women look their best in white—for instance, Lady Warwick, who wears an all-white costume, with white hat and gloves and shoes to match her white machine.

'Lady Archibald Campbell, an authority upon such subjects, has laid it down as a law that no costume can look equally well when walking and when upon wheels.

'The knicker-bocker pure and simple is a very unbecoming style, the short full bags which are seen in the Bois de Boulogne being quite incompatible with elegance and grace; but I have seen women look charming in these semi-manly garments when properly planned . . . For instance Lady Augusta Fane has worn a most becoming rational costume abroad. But what can be done with grace abroad is almost impossible in England, and here I have never seen anybody really looking well wearing anything but skirts.

'Mrs William James writes an amusing article about bicycling in the "Book of Beauty", and in this she points out very truly how the bicycle has come to be so carefully considered that no menial is entrusted with the task of putting it into the guard's van when travelling about, and now, when at home, it finds its home, not in the stables or any outbuilding, but in the hall itself. In the marble hall of Chelsea House, in Londonderry House, in Grosvenor House, and other most palatial mansions, the bicycle stand is now a matter of course, and many people, including Lady Evelyn Cobbold and Lady Henry FitzGerald, who both cycle well, are careful not to leave their machines exposed to the damp air and to dust without a cover. It is rather amusing to see a machine being wheeled along a platform snugly encased in its Crom-a-boo cover—a great protection from the scratches which so frequently disfigure a new coat of paint. Most women and many men have their machines painted in their own particular colours. Lady Huntingdon, for instance, has her machine painted green with primrose lines upon it; Miss Cornwallis West's colours are crimson and blue; Princess Henry of Plesse has the prettiest white machine that ever was seen; and no expense was spared in the finishing off of General Stracey's machine, which is done in the well-known red and blue of the Guards . . .

'The beginning of cycling was the end of the chaperon in England, and now women, even young girls ride alone or attended only by some casual man friend for miles together through deserted country roads. The danger of this is apparent; but parents and guardians will probably only become wise after the event. Given a lonely road, and a tramp desperate with hunger or naturally vicious, and it stands to reason that a girl, or indeed any woman, riding alone must be in some considerable peril'.

What a fearful chill that last paragraph must have set in the hearts of all Victorian mothers (mothers, that is, whose daughters were cyclists—but one supposes that the same danger lay in wait for non-cycling females as well). But what if your tramp desperate with hunger was also mounted on a bicycle? The mind boggles.

There is no doubt that the cycling craze spawned a host of melodramatic love stories—the cycling magazines of the 1880's are full of them. There is one in particular which appeared in one of the leading magazines in 1882. Called *A Ride For a Wife*, it tells of the awful plight of the true lovers Tom and Alice. Alice's father presses her to marry the rich but not terribly presentable Mr Haward, but her heart is with Tom. By a stroke of ill fate, Tom is sent abroad for two years on business. Alice's father intercepts Tom's love letters to her, and cold-heartedly destroys them. Alice, heartbroken at not hearing from Tom, eventually gives in to her father's wishes, and promises herself, wretched as she is, to Mr Haward. A date for the wedding has been fixed. Now read on.

'The wedding-morn has arrived, and already the bells of Nunwich Church are ringing out their joyous peals of gladness. But like a knell to her youth, like the burial-signal of the fresh young spring-tide of her life, sound they to the pale grief-stricken bride. Attended by her mother in her room, she pours out the wealth of her affection for Tom, and tells that her heart is slowly breaking, breaking under the weight of the awful step she is taking . . .

'But all is prepared and the procession of carriages, amidst the cheers of a large crowd, pass onwards towards the church. Factory girls stand by, with tears in their eyes, and envy the supposed happiness of the young bride. Ah! envy not; may-be that never in your life O! ye toilers of the loom, will ye e'er bear in your bosoms such a load of crushing sorrow as has now seized, with an everlasting clutch, upon the soul of that pale girl in yonder carriage.

'And, smiling and bowing by her side, sits the man to whose devilish pride this sin is due. Radiant with pleasure is he at the attainment of his wishes, and never a thought does he give to the ruin of the two lives he has so callously effected. But we will leave the bridal party to proceed towards the church, while we attempt to describe what is simultaneously taking place at Barmouth (Tom's home).

* * *

'In the small, but elegantly-appointed house fronting the sea, known throughout Barmouth as Ruston Villa, sat the family of that name at luncheon.

'"When do you expect Tom back, papa?" asked Kate Ruston, Tom's sister, who loved and worshipped her elder brother as if he were a demi-god, and resented the manner in which he had been treated by Alice's parents as only the sister of a jilted man can.

'"He should have been back last week," replied her father. "I cannot think what is detaining him."

'"I trust nothing has happened," anxiously interrupted his mother. '"By jove, isn't that his knock," shouted Harry, the younger son as a wave of rattling sound rolled through the house and caused all to start to their feet. "And, by the Lord! it is him," continued Harry as the dining-room door swung open and disclosed

Cyclists in the Belgian Army, 1914. (See Chapter 10)

British Army cyclists returning to the trenches, 1917, (See Chapter 10)

A section of the London District Signals Corps, March 1942.
(See Chapter 10)

our hero on the threshold . . . (Tom is welcomed home by all etc.).

'With a cold fear at her heart Mrs Ruston sat holding and softly stroking her son's hand, fearing that every instant he would make some enquiry as to Nunwich and the Kellys; and not long had she to wait. "Have you no news to tell me mother?", he asked: "You must know what is nearest to my heart, next to you. How is Alice? Have you seen her lately?"

'"I believe she is quite well," replied Mrs Ruston in a low voice.

'"But you are not sure, then?" interrupted Tom.

'"No, Tom," said his sister, laying her hand on his arm. "We are not sure—in fact we have not seen Miss Kelly for two months, and—"

'"Not seen her for two months, Katy? Mother, what does this mean? Tell me at once what has happened between you?"

'"I cannot, I cannot, my boy," replied Mrs Ruston, in tones broken with emotion.

'"Then, Mama, I will," said Kate. "Tom, my dear brother, is it possible that you do not know Miss Kelly is to be married, and that today?"

'"My God, what are you saying?" cried Tom, springing to his feet. "Only what is true, dear Tom; calm yourself for an instant, and listen to me while I tell you all."

'"Yes, yes, Kate, go on," answered her brother, setting his teeth and clenching his nails into the palms of his hands, in a determined effort to control his emotions. "But tell me quickly." (She tells him all about the wedding that day, of Alice to Haward . . .).

'"To Haward! Oh this is too cruel, and her *promise*," groaned Tom.

'"My brother," pursued his sister, "think no more of her; she is not worthy of such love as yours. Forget her utterly."

'"I cannot, I cannot," faltered Tom, "even now I would claim her if I could see her before she is irrevocably bound to that scoundrel, but there are no means of reaching her before that awful step is taken. Oh Alice, Alice," he moaned, "why would you not have faith?" and as these words passed his lips, a tear coursed down his cheek. No shame was there in that evidence of a heart-deep sorrow, naught at which the unfeeling could demur—for surely there is nothing so deeply affecting, so eminently grief-ful, as the riven tears of a strong man.

'"You could get there now, Tom, old boy," suddenly remarked, from a corner, his brother Harry, as all started at the sound of his voice. "You could get there now," he continued, "if you could spin a bit, as you did when you thrashed the beast for the Championship."

'"How, then?" quickly asked Tom.

'"Why ride, of course; your machine is all right, I have only been cleaning it this morning, and it is fit to go for a man's life."

'"God bless you, Harry," said Tom, "where is it?"

'"Go and slip into your togs," returned his brother, "you'll find 'em all in the old place, but they'll be rather tight. I'll have the crock ready. Sprint! You've got an hour and ten minutes to do the 15 miles and start."

'"I'll do it, or ride my heart out," replied Tom, as he vanished up the stairs. In a few moments he reappered clad in the uniform of the Barmouth Bicycle Club, his face white with the deadly pallor of a determination to risk all for the happiness of Alice and his own, for well he knew that he alone possessed her true affection.

'"Get up, Tom," said his brother, "you've no time to lose."

'"Now, Harry," cried Tom, and with a push off which would not have disgraced a Sopper or a Cortis, young Harry Ruston sent forward his brother upon that 15 mile ride, the issue of which was to brighten or begloom his fresh young life forever. Who could—or indeed would—essay to portray the conflicting emotions of our hero during his swift flight, which ever after marked an era in, and stood out in the past, as the turning point in his life. As he flew along the road what a tide of recollections rolled back on him—recollections once sweet as honey, now turned to the bitterness of gall as he fully realised the purpose of his present errand.

'But now, as the tenth milestone whirled by, he began to feel the want of that peculiar training, without which no man can hope to become a bicyclist pure and simple. His muscles felt like bars of iron, and his whole body ached with the violence of his exertions. Should he be in time—in time to avert that baleful union? The hills, those cruel rises, up which in the past he had so often shown the way, now appeared to be insurmountable. "Oh, for a lead, for a lead"!, he gasped, as he gained the summit of Horse Shoe Clump—the most trying on the road, and two miles from that church where he knew she now must be standing at the altar with the man who had, near this very spot, attempted his life in the dead of night, two years ago. Perhaps, by this time, she had become his wife, and lost to him forever. The thought was madness, death; and summoning all his remaining energies, he rushed the last mile down the straight to the church as if he was riding a London Handicap with the desperate energy of a scratch man. "Alice, Alice," he moaned, as, but two hundred yards from the gate, a sickening giddiness seized him, and he swerved dangerously across the road. With the energy of despair he steadied the machine, and, nearly fainting, fell rather than dismounted, before the church. The machine dropped with a clang on the roadway, and the crowd, awaiting in the churchyard the appearance of the bridal party, gazed with horror at the spectacle presented to them. A cyclist, whose features they knew not, covered with dust, his face a deadly whiteness, and utter exhaustion marking his features, was entering the church. As he gained the porch, so great was the silence that the words of the minister within were plainly audible. "Wilt thou have this man to thy wedded—"

'The door opened with a crash, and all within rose to their feet at the interruption. Up the aisle rushed Tom, with a cry of "Alice, I am here," his arms outstretched towards the veiled figure at the altar.

' "Tom!," and with a piercing cry the girl swooned in her father's arms . . .'

And, so, they lived happily ever after, the dastardly Haward having been thwarted. Heady stuff. Or, as Oscar Wilde said about the death of Little Nell, 'it would take a man with a real heart of stone not to die laughing'.

Nowadays, of course, it's all done with sports cars and such like. But in Ireland, the bicycle is still used a great deal for courting, especially in the rural areas. This, no doubt, is what gave rise to the following story.

Sean O'Boyle was a man of small stature and quiet nature. But he had one fault. He was not the most rigorous of men at attending to his religious duties. For years, so many that he could not remember their number, he had not been to confession. But at last, one day, under great pressure from his wife, and for the sake of the children, he repented. That evening he slipped into an empty church, and into the confessional. The priest arrived a moment or two later. 'Bless me, father, for I have sinned,' he intoned automatically. The priest, as is the wont of priests hearing confession, seemed to be taking little notice. 'I have the most awful sins to confess, father,' continued Sean. The old priest hardly moved. He was used to this sort of thing. 'I have committed adultery, father.' 'How many times,' growled the priest, shooting a discreet glance through the grille. 'I've lost count, father.' There was a pause. 'The same woman?' asked the priest. 'Well, no, father . . . the truth is—I have forty-three mistresses—' 'Forty-three mistresses!' The priest's eyes opened a little. 'And ninety-four illegitimate children,' continued Sean. The priest was truly amazed so much so that he dropped all pretence of avuncularity. He stood up in his cubicle, and looked at Sean's puny frame. 'Great thundering Hokey,' exclaimed the priest, 'how in under God do ye do it, man?', showing a most unpriestly interest in man's sexual prowess.

'Well, father, ye see, I have a bicycle . . .'

10

'BOMB THEIR BIKES'

On Friday, 3rd of October, 1967, a London evening newspaper carried the following report.

'Washington, Friday. Senator William Fulbright, chairman of the United States Foreign Relations Committee, has a new plan to force Hanoi to peace talks: Bombing bicycles instead of bridges in North Vietnam.

'The senator made the suggestion when Harrison Salisbury of the New York Times told a committee that Communist supplies were hauled to South Vietnam on bicycles.

'Said Mr Salisbury, who recently visited Hanoi: "I literally believe that without bikes they'd have to get out of the war".

'Remarked Senator Fulbright: "Why don't we concentrate on bicycles instead of bridges? Does the Pentagon know about this?"'

What would appear on the surface to be a light-hearted remark, actually gives the clue to the American predicament in Vietnam. The war in Vietnam is essentially a guerilla war. And the American attempt to win it with sophisticated weapons and advanced, or so-called advanced strategy, is a fruitless one.

A guerilla war must be fought with guerilla tactics—a bicycle is of more use in the jungle than a tank. This, the French found to their cost when they were routed at Dien Bien Phu by the Viet Minh in 1954. However, more about that later.

It is ironical that it was a war which gave England the chance to catch up with the French in the development of the bicycle. When the Franco-Prussian War broke out in 1870, France was already years ahead of any other country with the design and manufacture of the bicycle. This was cut short in 1870, and England took the lead, as has been explained in a previous chapter.

Soon after that, the military, sometimes slow in adopting new machines (during the First World War, most of the British High Command laughed the idea of mechanised war to scorn, and during the tail-end of the Second World War, one British general was prepared to line up his tanks for a cavalry charge), began to tap the potential of the bicycle as a military tool. An article in *The Illustrated War News* of February, 1917, gives some key dates:

'The introduction of the military cyclist appears to date from 1875. Italy first employed them during the manoeuvres of that year for carrying mesages. Ten years later, in 1885, armed cyclists were used by Colonel Tamplin as scouts during the Easter manoeuvres in England. The whole outfit, including the rifle weighed about 56 lb. In 1886, the French used military cyclists as despatch riders.

'The Austrians in 1896 and the French military authorities in 1898 carried the development of the military cycle a step further by introducing a machine which could be folded and carried on its rider's back in an emergency. The folding bicycles weighed about 28 lb.'

A note of pride is evident in the following extract from *His Majesty's Territorial Army, Volume 3*, by Walter Richards, published in 1909:

'The 25th (County of London) Cyclist Battalion the London Regiment deserves special notice as representing the premier Cyclist Battalion, not only in this country, but, it is believed, in the world. The date of its formation was 1888, when it was raised as the 26th Middlesex 'Cyclist Volunteer Rifle Corps, its first commanding officer, and in a sense, its originator, being Colonel Savile, who, up to that time had been professor of tactics at the Royal Staff College, Camberley. At first the establishment of the corps was the modest one of 121 of all ranks, which, however, before long, was increased to 361. The corps was for some time attached to the 2nd South Middlesex. The experiment, started in 1900, of Cyclist Companies as integral parts of the Volunteer battalions proved somewhat of an obstacle to the 26th recruiting its full numbers, and for some years it did not much exceed fifty per cent of the establishment.

'But before long the authorities began to incline towards the battalion organisation. The well-remembered Cyclist Manoeuvres of 1906, at which fifty Cyclist Companies were represented by, on an average, forty from each Company (the 26th supplying five of its officers to staff appointments), proved to quote one of the leading authorities on military cycling, beyond question "the inadequacy of the Cyclist Company organisation for combined work".

'The following year Colonel Gilbertson Smith, then commanding the 26th and now the 25th Cyclist Battalion, and who, it has been said, had at that time "done more to develop military cycling than any other man in England", was authorised to bring the strength of his command up to 500 by adding to it certain specified Cyclist Companies, and in the manoeuvres that followed the advantages of the system were triumphantly shown'.

Of course, on large scale, text-book military operations, the bicycle is not much use. A soldier cycling is a sitting target, and is virtually unarmed. But the bicycle comes into its own in unconventional operations, such as the Boer War. This is made clear in a history of the Boer War called *With the Flag to Pretoria* by H. W. Wilson:

'The cycle and the road locomotive have both been largely used in this war, for the first time, and both have fully justified their inclusion in the Army's equipment. In a land where the mortality among horses has been so great, the ever-ready cycle has been of great value. . . .'

Later in the same book Wilson has this to say; in a caption to a photograph:

'Lord Edward Cecil's Cadet Corps boy orderlies, who play a prominent part in the siege of Mafeking—They ranged from nine years old to fifteen or sixteen, used donkeys and bicycles, and became quite expert in dodging shells.'

It was the invention of the pneumatic tyre which gave the bicycle a real fillip as a potential military tool. In 1896, a Captain R. E. Thompson, of the Signal Corps of the United States Army, saw the possibilities of using the bicycle for laying and retrieving temporary telegraph and telephone wires. He invented an attachment which was tested by running a length of wire over a third of a mile, and reeling it back in a total time of two minutes. In 1887 an experiment was tried at the Northwestern Military Academy at Lake Geneva, Wisconsin. An officer organised a corps of sixteen cadets with sixteen standard bicycles equipped with clips for rifles and other military gear. Wall scaling was one of the tests carried out by the cyclists. In one test, a wall of 16 feet was scaled by the team, carrying their bicycles, etc., all in the space of three minutes. The same officer also developed a motorised tricycle equipped with a machine gun and seats for four cadets. The United States Army commissioned the Pope manufacturing company to develop a bicycle on which was mounted a Colt automatic machine gun. Pope also produced for the army a tandem equipped with a twelve-shot repeating rifle, two Colt quick-action revolvers, a case of signal flags, two rolled overcoats and two rolled blankets.

At the outbreak of the Boer War, Pedersen, the man who designed the famous Dursley Pedersen bicycle, designed a folding model weighing only 15 lb., which could be carried on the back across the shoulders. During the First World War, the folding bicycle was used widely by all sides. The folding model was also used in the Second World War, especially by paratroops, but was not terribly successful. A British War Department film, made during the Second War, warned civilians to be always on the look-out for German troops in disguise. A shot in the film shows a German soldier dressed as a nun, who suddenly whips a folding bicycle from under 'her' habit, assembles it, and rides off! By God, those Germans were a cunning lot.

Of course, once the bicycle had been accepted by the British Army, regulations had to be drawn up for its use in the field of battle and in drilling and ceremonial occasions. The first book of regulations was drawn up in 1907, revised in 1911 and, no doubt, revised occasionally ever since. Issued by the General Staff, published by HMSO, price sixpence, the preface says: 'This manual is issued by command of the Army Council, and deals with the training of cyclists and their leading in war.' Regulation 64 deals with saluting:

'A cyclist standing with his cycle, with rifle attached to it, will salute with the right hand, as laid down in Section 19, returning the hand to the point of the saddle on the completion of the salute. When at ease, a cyclist, whether mounted or leading his cycle, will salute by coming to attention, and turning his head to the officer he salutes. A party of cyclists on the march will salute on the command Eyes Right, which will be followed by Eyes Front, from the officer or NCO in charge.'

This is the sort of stuff which renders the bicycle almost useless in the type of warfare at which it is best. But the army is the army, and everything has got to be regulated. Regulation 65 tells us:

'The position of the cyclist at attention is the same as that of the dismounted soldier, except that he will grasp the left steering handle with his left hand, and place the right hand at the point of the saddle, elbow to the rear.'

A very difficult position if the cyclist happens to be standing on the right of the bicycle. The order to ground and take up cycles, is even more rigorous:

'Ground cycles. Take a place of 30 inches to the left, place the bicycle carefully on the ground and come to attention. Note: Cycles, unless fitted with a service-pattern lamp or one of similar design, should not be grounded unless the lamps are removed.

'Take up cycles. Raise the bicycle, take a pace of 30 inches to the right and come to attention.'

One can at least say this for the army—their regulations were thorough if nothing else. There is even a regulation on stacking of bicycles:

'Stack cycles. On the command Cycles, odd numbers will move round in rear of and to the right side of their cycles, and each file will incline their cycles towards each other. The front wheels will be turned outward, the handlebars interlocked, and the men will stand to attention. Rifles must always be detached before stacking cycles; they can be piled, or preferably placed against the saddles of the cycles.

'Unstack cycles. On the command Cycles, each man will grasp his cycle and unlock the handlebars.'

But for real thoroughness, there is even a regulation on mounting the bicycle, but less specific than the others:

'The cyclist mounts or dismounts in the manner to which he is accustomed, the quickest method to do so being from the pedal.'

Really? However, we get some action when the regulations come to the section on tactical action:

'Cyclists can be used to the best advantage where the roads and paths are good and numerous, for, under these conditions, they will be able to move quickly to the point where their intervention in the fight is required, to deploy rapidly, and to move again to a fresh position rapidly, should necessity arise. The power of rapid movement in a favourable country enables the cyclist to act suddenly from any direction more quickly than infantry. They can thus deceive the enemy as to the nature and strength of the force by which he is opposed and are therefore endowed with relatively greater staying power. It follows that the chief factors necessary to bring about successful tactical action of cyclists are: (1) Favourable country, which allows rapidity of movement and surprise. (2) Rapid deployment, and the immediate development of full strength and fire power, which mystify the enemy, and cause him to hesitate and delay.'

And here's another cunning tip:

'In cases where it is not necessary to move far away from the bicycles, every man may be used in the firing line. But when the men are required to make a long advance on foot after dismounting, as usually occurs when an outflanking movement across country is undertaken, it will often be necessary to leave half the men with the bicycles to bring them on later. Every effort must be made to avoid sending the men back long distances to fetch their machines.'

The army misses nothing. How's this for a regulation?

'Bicycle tyres should be wiped with a damp cloth after a march, so that all grit, which if left might cause a puncture, may be removed.'

Another one covers the rate of marching etc.:

'The rate of marching, excluding halts, will generally vary from 8 to 10 miles per hour, according to the weather, the nature of the country, and the state of the roads. A column of battalion size should not be expected to cover more than 50 miles in a day under favourable conditions.'

But for a real gem, read the last paragraph of the following regulation:

'The first object of cyclists in an attack, is to bring every available rifle to bear at once. In close country, therefore, where suitable parallel roads exist, it will usually be convenient to march on more than one road. Moreover, it is more difficult for the enemy to surprise several columns, than one, and conversely, it is easier to find out his weak point and concentrate against it.

'All ranks of cyclist units employed in coast defence should be trained in the use of the telephone.'

In spite of the fact that England has never been invaded since 1066, the army were obviously not taking any chances. This is also reflected in the following regulation:

'In order to fulfil their role of delaying the enemy's advance, cyclist battalions must be familiar with areas which lend themselves to delaying action. They must ascertain by careful reconnaissance how the defensive capabilities of such positions can be improved and what local materials are available for the purpose. Rallying to selected rendezvous from look-out stations should be practised both by day and by night. Should an enemy succeed in landing, cyclist patrols should at once establish pickets on all roads radiating from the landing place. The duties of these patrols will be to keep in close touch with the enemy to ascertain and report his movements, and to prevent his reconnoitring parties from getting through.'

As has been pointed out, the bicycle works best in guerilla warfare, and especially in rough country, in spite of what the army regulations say. It was used by the IRA in Ireland during the War of Independence against the English. (Between the two world wars, the regular Irish army had a cavalry regiment mounted entirely on bicycles.) A cyclist on a dark night with no lights is fast and unobtrusive. And, of course, all sorts of secret documents can be smuggled around, stuffed down the tubular handlebars or the frame.

But for the most dramatic use of bicycles, we must turn to the Japanese invasion of Malaya and the fall of Singapore in 1942. General Yamashita had prepared his ground well. He already had set up a network of espionage and intelligence, recruiting Japanese fishermen, plantation managers, merchants, barbers and photographers, long before he set foot in Malaya in December 1941. So, he had a very good idea of what was going on before he got there. This was one of the reasons for his defeat of Percival's army, which was three times the size of his own, numerically.

One of the ironies of that whole campaign, is that it was a stock exercise at British Staff Colleges long before the war—and each year, the students agreed that the best way to subdue Singapore would be to land in Malaya and head south. Each year, students in the Tokyo War College also arrived at the same conclusion. Unfortunately, Britain did not learn any lessons from the exercise but the Japanese did.

Before the invasion, Yamashita trained his men on Hainan Island in conditions similar to those in Malaya. They lived rough, they carried out numerous landings, and they learned to travel with the minimum of equipment. Each of his men was given a booklet giving hints on health matters in Malaya's humid atmosphere, and how to live off the land.

One of the secrets of the bicycle's success is that it does not require specially built tracks, and it only takes up a width of eighteen inches unloaded. And this is a quality that Yamashita used in his invasion of Malaya. His troops used bicycles and abandoned British trucks for transport, and trekked through jungle thought by the British to be impenetrable simply because it had never been penetrated before. Yamashita's troops also used the bicycle to give the impression that they had a lot more troops than they actually had. They rode through the jungle on the machines, holding fire crackers and fireworks which made one hell of a din. The result was that the British thought the jungle was teeming with Japanese, and conseqently withdrew.

The importance of these tactics was not lost on the insurgent guerilla army of Ho Chi Minh and General Vo Nguyen Giap in French Indo-China, which the Japanese had invaded when France fell to the Nazis.

When the Second World War ended, the French once more

took over Indo-China, but were hotly resisted by the Viet Minh. After 1945, the Viet Minh slowly built up an army, and trained it in the tactics of guerilla warfare as laid down by Mao Tse Tung in his various writings on his own campaigns. (It might be appropriate to quote one or two of Mao's thoughts on this score: 'With the common people of the whole country mobilised we shall create a vast sea of humanity and drown the enemy in it'—and—'The people are the sea and the guerilla fighter is the fish'.) With only limited means and resources, General Giap had to move slowly and modestly at first. But his army grew, and with it, the resistance to the French. Transport was a problem; the lines of communication are very important for the transport of the two basics—food and ammunition—for any battle over the size of a minor skirmish. But the lesson of the Japanese bicycles was not lost on Giap. He built up a complex system of porters who, both on foot and especially with bicycles, helped in the battles against the French. Giap has revealed an interesting statistic about one major battle against the French which was fought in January 1951. It lasted five days, and during that time over 5,000 tons of rice and ammunition were brought into the battle zone by porters, about 180,000 of whom had been either directly or indirectly involved in the campaign!

But the campaign which finally forced the French to surrender was the battle of Dien Bien Phu in 1954—out of which the present war in Vietnam was born. The French strategy was simple if nothing else. General Navarre, then Commander-in-Chief of French Indo-China, set up a centre of resistance at Dien Bien Phu to attract and hold the attention of the Viet Minh divisions gathered round the Laos border. The purpose of this was twofold: to prevent a Viet Minh invasion of Laos, and to prevent the Viet Minh divisions being used against the French forces defending the Delta. Further, Navarre argued, if the Viet Minh attacked the Dien Bien Phu fortress complex (actually a series of fortresses, they would not only be repulsed, but repeated attacks and defeats would sap their morale, their ammunition, and their food. Also, Navarre argued, if the Viet Minh did not attack but try to by-pass the position, the French could go into the jungle and harass them, always returning to their strong base. The French Air Force could also cut off the Viet Minh supply lines.

The basic flaws in this thinking were in underestimating the number of divisions of the Viet Minh there were in the hills surrounding the fortress, the amount of heavy artillery they had installed there, and the number and nature of lines of communication which had been set up for the transport of ammunition and food, And it was in the supply and communication set-up that the bicycle played its biggest part. With the help of thousands of porters and thousands of bicycles, ammunition and rice were transported through the jungle and stockpiled around the Dien Bien Phu complex for months before the battle was joined. In spite of using napalm, the French Air Force could not pin-point the almost invisible lines of bicycles, threading through the jungle, each carrying as much as 500 lb. of supplies.

On March 10, 1954, Viet Minh guns shelled the French airstrip for the first time, causing dismay in the French camps, since it was the sole means of exit for the garrison. But on March 13, the first real attack began, with an assault by the Viet Minh on the outlying French defended posts. Three of these posts fell to the Viet Minh. Another major attack was made on March 30, and lasted until April 4. Dien Bien Phu was completely encircled. Now Giap tightened the noose. From April 5 to May 1, the Viet Minh sapped their way steadily forward, digging trenches as they went, a method startlingly like the methods of the First World War. On May 1, the final series of assaults on Dien Bien Phu began. On May 7, around noon, a Viet Minh division broke right into the heart of the French defences; by nightfall it was all over. Although the Viet Minh had lost a lot of men, the French had paid dearly for underestimating the numbers involved, the ferocious fighting spirit of their enemy and, though a small detail, still important—the use of the bicycle as a means of transport for war. The final irony of the battle of Dien Bien Phu is that the Viet Minh were using French bicycles—made by Peugeot!

Vietnam: a people's transport column in South Vietnam. This was one of the transport techniques used by the Viet Minh to defeat the French at Dien Bien Phu. (See Chapter 10)

A shot of Jacques Tati from his film 'Jour de Fete'. (See Chapter 11)

11

SYMBOL OF THE ANTI-HERO

'Look fairly and see clearly. Of the two wheels of this machine, which possesses the unmarred symbolism which denotes the Hub of Man, the Spokes of pre-History, the Rim of Medievalism, the Tyres of Civilisation? It is the first wheel, the former wheel, the wheel which both leads and commands; in its simple grandeur it may be called the true image of Man's Estate. This is the famous wheel of fire, the prayer-wheel of the Tibetans, the wheel of St. Catherine, the wheel of fate. In the rear wheel we see a meaner revelation—Man enchained with chains of grit and oil, driven not by love, not by ambition, but by the most ignoble and ludicrous, sparsely-haired and sweating, malodorous and malformed parts of the human body; I mean the feet.'

ADRIAN MITCHELL.
(*If You See Me Comin'*)

If the automobile is the vehicle and, indeed, the symbol of the hero in modern literature, then the bicycle is the symbol of the anti-hero. If we thrill to, and envy, the adventures of James Bond in his racy, pacy sports cars, then we are reassured and smile at the hero (or anti-hero) of John Wain's *Hurry on Down* as he cycles to work. This is a false cosiness—dispelled by the aggressiveness and determination with which Arthur Seaton in the film of Alan Sillitoe's *Saturday Night and Sunday Morning* cycles to work at a factory. Wain's hero (anti) is a graduate who is merely playing at being a manual worker, whereas Seaton *is* a manual worker, trapped in a prison of a Midlands factory—but the ubiquitous bicycle serves both of these author's purposes; Wain's, to add colour to an already picaresque character; Sillitoe's, to point up the character of the instinctive anarchist Seaton.

However, to begin at the beginning. The first recorded use of the bicycle in the arts was in 1804, amazingly enough. In that year, a comedy called *Les Velociferes* was produced at the Vaudville Theatre, Paris. No doubt it was a satire on the craze of the young bucks of the Directory, the Incroyables, who, it may be remembered, made great sport of riding around on the early bicycles which were called velociferes. (Incidentally, is there a play based on the motor-car, or the steam engine?) No copy of the play was available at the time of writing this book, but it is interesting that the (then) new invention inspired someone to construct a drama around the whole affair. Aside from that play, and in spite of the torrent of literary mush produced around and inspired by the bicycle (especially during the Victorian period, as has already been illustrated in an earlier chapter), we have to wait another ninety years for the first definitive and serious work of art inspired by the bicycle. This is H. G. Well's *Wheels of Chance*. Written in 1896, the main character is a draper's assistant called Hoopdriver. He is a bit of a weedy character given to day dreaming and romanticising about his own life, which in reality is dull, humdrum and boring, to say the least. In fact, Hoopdriver could easily have been the model for the later Walter Mitty, the James Thurber character. Around Hoopdriver, Wells has constructed a beautiful little comedy and satire on the social snobberies of the period, the New Women of the 1890's, the plight of overworked and underpaid drapers' assistants, and, of course, the new craze of cycling. Wells must have been a keen cyclist himself. Here is his description of Hoopdriver's first cycling holiday:

'The Glory of Holidays had resumed its sway with a sudden accession of splendour. At the crest of the hill he puts his feet upon the foot-rests, and now riding moderately straight, went, with a palpitating brake, down that excellent descent. A new delight was in his eyes, quite over and above the pleasure of rushing through the keen, sweet, morning air. He reached out his thumb and twanged his bell out of sheer happiness.'

The whole action of the novel takes place during Hoopdriver's annual holiday. His day-dreams come true, and he actually ends up rescuing a damsel in distress. However, after many adventures cycling around the south of England, they part, she to return to her step-mother, he to return to the drudgery of the draper's shop. But on setting out for his holiday, there is no lack of advice from his fellow workers:

'Briggs had never been on a bicycle in his life, but he felt Hoopdriver's inexperience and offered such advice as occurred to him. "Have the machine thoroughly well-oiled," said Briggs; "carry one or two lemons with you; don't tear yourself to death the first day, and sit upright. Never lose control of the machine, and always sound the bell on every possible occasion" '.

And, of course, Hoopdriver, a beginner as far as cycling is concerned, has to have a few secret practice rides before setting out. And Wells extracts a lot of fun out of this:

'Now, the reader may be inclined to wonder how a respectable young shopman could have got his legs, and indeed himself generally into such a dreadful condition. One might fancy that he had been sitting with his nether regions in some complicated machinery, a threshing-machine, say, or one of those hay-making furies. But Sherlock Holmes (now, after a glorious career, happily and decently dead) would have fancied nothing of the kind. He would have recognised at once that the bruises on the internal aspect of the left leg, considered in the light of the distribution of the other abrasions and contusions, pointed unmistakably to the violent impact of the Mounting Beginner upon the bicycling saddle, and that the ruinous state of the right knee was equally eloquent of the concussions attendant on that person's hasty, frequently causeless, and invariably ill-conceived descents.'

Wells's novel is peppered with a host of minor characters, who invariably meet Hoopdriver in hotels or on the road. Here is an ebullient clergyman:

'"You are, I perceive, cycling through this delightful country," said the clergyman. "Touring," explained Hoopdriver. "I can imagine that, with a properly oiled machine, there can be no easier nor pleasanter way of seeing the country." "No," said Mr Hoopdriver; "it isn't half a bad way of getting about."

'"For a young and newly married couple, a tandem bicycle must be, I should imagine, a delightful bond," "Quite so," said Hoopdriver, reddening a little. "Do you ride a tandem?" "No—we're separate," said Hoopdriver. "The motion through the air is indisputably of a very exhilarating description . . . I myself am a cyclist," said the clergyman, suddenly descending upon Mr Hoopdriver; "we are all cyclists nowadays," with a broad smile.'

Wells, being the Socialist that he was, obviously approved, like Georges Sorel, of the bicycle as the great equaliser. In spite of that, however, an earlier passage in the novel recounts an abrasive meeting with a heath-keeper:

'"They're trying things, them bicycles," said the heath-keeper charitably. "Very trying." Mr Hoopdriver gave the nut a vicious turn, and suddenly stood up—he was holding the front wheel between his knees. "I wish," said he, with a catch in his voice, "I wish you'd leave off staring at me." Then, with the air of one who has delivered an ultimatum, he began replacing the screw-hammer in the wallet.

'The heath-keeper never moved. Possibly he raised his eyebrows, and certainly he stared harder than he did before. "You're pretty unsociable," he said slowly, as Mr Hoopdriver seized the handles and stood ready to mount as soon as the cart had passed . . . "Can't no one make a passing remark to you, Touchy? Ain't I good enough to speak to you?"

'Mr Hoopdriver stared into the Immensity of the Future. He was rigid with emotion. It was like abusing the Lions in Trafalgar Square. But the heath-keeper felt his honour was at stake. "Don't you make no remarks to 'im," said he as the carter came up broadside. " 'E's a bloomin' dook, 'e is. 'E don't converse with no one under a earl . . ." '

Hoopdriver is nonplussed by this encounter, but rides off very shakily on his bicycle, surely the archtype anti-hero of all time.

Another famous novelist, a contemporary of Wells, was Jerome K. Jerome, whose best-known book is *Three Men in a Boat*. Jerome wrote a sequel to that work—called *Three Men on the Bummel*; it concerned the same three heroes, but this time on a bicycle tour. Written in the usual inimitable style, it will suffice here to give one or two quotations for a flavour of the style. The three heroes, George, Harris and J—, discuss the nature of the tour which they are planning. Someone suggests a bicycle tour. This gives the author an excuse to launch into meditation on the peculiar difficulties of sharing a tandem bicycle:

'There is always unpleasantness about this tandem. It is the theory of the man in front that the man behind does nothing; it is equally the theory of the man behind that he alone is the motive power, the man in front merely doing the puffing. The mystery will never be solved. It is annoying when Prudence is whispering to you on the one side not to overdo your strength and bring on heart disease; while Justice into the other ear is remarking, "Why should you do it all? This isn't a cab. He's not your passenger,": to hear him grunt out:

' "What's the matter—lost your pedals?" '

But the funniest passage in the book is a dissertation on the bicycle as a means of exercise. The author has just described how a friend had completely wrecked a bicycle of his, by 're-pairing' it: He continues:

'"There are two ways you can get exercise out of a bicycle: you can "overhaul" it, or you can ride it. On the whole, I am not sure that man who takes his pleasure overhauling does not get the best of the bargain. He is independent of the weather and the wind; the state of the roads troubles him not. Give him a screw-hammer, a bundle of rags, an oil-can, and something to sit down upon, and he is happy for the day. He has to put up with certain disadvantages, of course; there is no joy without alloy. He himself always looks like a tinker, and his machine always suggests the idea that, having stolen it, he has tried to disguise it; but as he rarely goes beyond the first milestone with it, this, perhaps, does not much matter. The mistake some people make is in thinking that you can get both forms of sport out of the same machine. This is impossible; no machine will stand the double strain. You must make up your mind whether you are going to be an "overhauler" or a rider. Personally, I prefer to ride, therefore I take care to have near me nothing that can tempt me to overhaul. When anything happens to my machine I wheel it to the nearest repair shop. If I am too far from the town or village, I sit down by the roadside and wait till a cart comes along. My chief danger, I find, is the wandering overhauler. The sight of a broken-down machine is to the overhauler as a wayside corpse to a crow; he swoops down on it with a friendly yell of triumph."'

With the advent of the motor-car, the bicycle fell out of popularity with writers as a vehicle in both senses of the word. And it was not until after the Second World War that it began to creep into the works of novelists and poets. The reason for that is obvious. In a country at war, motor-cars and especially petrol and diesel fuel are at a premium. The bicycle comes momentarily back into its own, people's memories are jolted, and the bicycle becomes the symbol of earlier, happier days—a key opening up a great reservoir of nostalgia (as, for example, in some of the poems of John Betjeman). In this respect, perhaps one of the most ambitious projects ever embarked upon, and based on the bicycle, was a film operetta called *Me And*

My Bike by the Welsh poet, Dylan Thomas. Unfortunately he died before he finished it. In a foreword to the published portion, Mr Sydney Box, explained how Thomas himself described the project:

'"I want to write the first original *film operetta*," he told me. 'It will be all about a man who loves a bicycle. It's called Me And My Bike and it covers the whole span of this man's life. He rides pennyfarthings, tandems, tricycles, racing bikes—and when he dies at the end, he rides on his bike up a sunbeam straight to heaven, where he's greeted by a heavenly chorus of bicycle bells."'

The film was to be in five major sequences, each sequence being a decade of years. The published portion contains only the first sequence. It is a shame Thomas never lived to finish it, for it promises well. The hero is called Augustus, the heroine, Georgina. Georgina lives in a country mansion—a very horsey mansion—with a gruff horse-loving father, a very timid mother, and a real dragon of a grand-mother—also a fanatical horse-lover. (Interesting to note that Thomas writes the script in a fashion which makes it eminently readable for both the layman and the professional film director—a technique which Thomas was just beginning to explore, and which was later on successfully exploited by Arthur Miller in the film script which he wrote for Marilyn Monroe—*The Misfits.*) The big snag about Augustus, as far as the family are concerned, is that he rides a bicycle—and, (at this stage) a penny-farthing at that! However, Georgina and Augustus meet, while the rest of the family are out horse riding The butler and the footmen of the household do not take kindly to storing Augustus's bicycle away—'Take this Hobject away,' 'it's a heysore to horsemen'—'Take this error away, To 'orsmen it's 'ell.'—'Take this 'otch potch away. It's a insult to 'orseflesh.'—'Take this engine away. All bicycles smell'—and so on.

But Georgina and Augustus are unabashed, and break into a duet:

GEORGINA: How stern you appear
With your penny-farthen,
Augustus my dear,
So imposing astride it
And not scared a bit
Oh I'd have a fit
If I even tried it!
AUGUSTUS: For you I would ride it
Georgina, my dear,
From here to Carmarthen.
GEORGINA: Oh how brave you are then
On your penny-farthen!
AUGUSTUS: Though it is, I admit,
Very sharp where you sit.
GEORGINA: How impressively you pedal!
AUGUSTUS: How excessively it shakes!
GEORGINA: Your monster made of metal
AUGUSTUS: And every whisker aches.
GEORGINA: How aggressively you pedal!
AUGUSTUS: Though it hasn't any brakes.

They say the gods dislike disillusionment. Thomas never finished his film operetta. But another genius did actually complete a film about the bicycle—Buster Keaton. The film—*Our Hospitality*—made in 1923, features the dead-pan-faced Keaton riding a very early bicycle, which he called a gentleman's hobbyhorse, along a rural hamlet crossroads in farming country in 1831. Keaton ironically anticipates present-day New York's traffic problems—he comes racing up to the crossroads on the hobbyhorse and a local constable holds him up to let a horse and wagon pass across. That particular hobbyhorse, specially built for the film from an old print, is itself preserved in the Smithsonian Institution in Washington.

But no-one has enchanted as much humour out of a bicycle in films as Jacques Tati, that marvellous French mime, comedian and artist. In his film, *Jour de Fete*, he uses the bicycle as an indispensable prop in the part he plays as the village postman in post-Second War France. It is impossible to describe in prose how he achieves it, and to attempt it would be foolish. But it is probably true to say that what he achieves is the logical extension of the silent film art of Max Linder and Charlie Chaplin. Tati is the true inheritor of these artists' legacy, and, by imaginative investment, has made it appreciate ten-fold. But one must see *Jour de Fete* to feel the real gold.

But not all novelists have used the bicycle as a humorous vehicle. The Italian novelist, Luigi Bartolini, in his searing book *Bicycle Thieves*,* describes the back streets and slums of post-war Rome. Again, significantly, the book was written around 1950—but in this novel, unlike Dylan Thomas's poetic treatment, the bicycle is an absolute necessity for the narrator. The story is simple. The narrator, who is never named, is searching for his bicycle, which has been stolen by a gang of young petty hooligans. During his searches, he meditates, sometimes bitterly, sometimes tenderly, on the vile teeming slums which crawl with greed, corruption, cruelty, and, above all, poverty:

'The square is crowded from morning until night, so much so that it is impossible to move except with the greatest difficulty—crowded with thieves of every class and creed, who steal every object imaginable; yard goods, leggings, shoes, lamps and cords, even toothbrushes and perfumes, razors and razor blades, inner tubes and patches, clocks, and above all, bicycles . . . Here can be found shiny new Bianchis with lamp brackets, the latest model. For the lamp alone they ask three thousand lire. A twenty eight and three quarters tyre sells for twenty nine hundred lire, and a twenty eight and five eighths tyre sells for thirty two hundred lire. Here can be seen thieves who carry, bandolier-fashion, bundles of inner tubes and quantities of tyres. Others have spread dirty blankets on the ground at the far end of the Piazzetta, and on top of them display parts of stolen and dismantled bicycles, for the first thing that is done to a bicycle is to dismantle or camouflage it.'

After this initial description, albeit general, later in the novel

* Original edition published in Italy by Longanesi & Co., Milan, English edition published by Michael Joseph Ltd.

the narrator launches into a bitter tirade against the authorities, using his stolen bicycle as a launching pad:

'Surely by now they have dismantled it, piece by piece, bolt by bolt, screw by screw, I continued to lament. And today they will begin by selling one of the handlebar grips, and tomorrow the other. Or perhaps they won't even do it this way . . . not today, not tomorrow, but who knows in how many months, and who knows where! Can you after a year remember the colour and shape of the handlebars of a bicycle that has been stolen from you? And yet I should be able to remember even a fragment that belonged to my bicycle. One can do anything, but with a police force that does nothing to stop thieves, and perhaps even shows them what they should do, you may as well give up all hope of finding your bicycle again. In extreme cases they may keep the thieves in hand in order to use them against anti-Fascists, if the Fascists should return, or against the Fascists if the anti-Fascists stay.'

Bartolini's novel was eventually made into a film in the late fifties—a film which won not only critical acclaim but many international prizes.

Bartolini uses the bicycle as a hinge on which to hang, like a decorated panel, a descriptive door to the post-war, poverty-ridden Rome. But there is another writer who uses the bicycle in his works, not so much as a hinge, or a pivot, but an integral part of the characters whom he describes, using it even, perhaps, as a symbol of the intractability of things. That writer is Samuel Beckett, who created a turning point, a true breakthrough in world theatre with his play *Waiting For Godot*. *Waiting For Godot* shook Western theatre out of its lethargy, and literature has never been the same since. Although the bicycle never appears nor is mentioned in that particular play, the mention of it in this book is relevant, since it gives the clue to Beckett's particular vision and genius. In *Godot*, silence, for the first time, became as important on the stage as spoken dialogue. A man's silences, Beckett is saying, are as much a part of a man's psyche as his spoken words, perhaps even more so. So is his hat, so is his overcoat, so is his boot, so is his baldness, so is his blindness, so is his deafness, so (to get to the point) is his bicycle. Beckett is never too explicit—explicitness is the enemy of lucidity. In his radio play *All That Fall* (radio is one of Beckett's favourite media), he uses both the silences, and the sounds of the countryside for maximum effect. Mrs Rooney is making her way to the railway station along a country road. Mr Tyler approaches on his bicycle:

Sound of dragging feet. (Mrs Rooney's) Sound of bicycle bell. It is old Mr Tyler coming up behind her on his bicycle, on his way to the station. Squeak of brakes. He slows down and rides abreast of her.

MR TYLER: Mrs Rooney! Pardon me if I do not doff my cap, I'd fall off. Divine day for the meeting.

MRS ROONEY: Oh, Mr Tyler, you startled the life out of me stealing up behind me like a deer-stalker. Oh!

MR TYLER: (*Playfully*) I rang my bell, Mrs Rooney, the moment I sighted you I started tinkling my bell, now don't you deny it.

MRS ROONEY: Your bell is one thing, Mr Tyler, and you are another. What news of your poor daughter?

MR TYLER: Fair, fair. They removed everything, you know, the whole . . . er . . . bag of tricks. Now I am grandchildless. (*Sound of dragging feet.*)

MRS ROONEY: Gracious how you wobble! Dismount, for mercy's sake, or ride on.

MR TYLER: Perhaps if I were to lay my hand lightly on your shoulder, Mrs Rooney, how would that be? (*Pause*) Would you permit that?

MRS ROONEY: No, Mr Rooney, Mr Tyler, I mean, I am tired of light old hands on my shoulders and other senseless places, sick and tired of them. Heavens, here comes Connolly's van! (*She halts. Sound of motor van. It approaches, passes with thunderous rattle, recedes.*) Are you all right, Mr Tyler? (*Pause*) Where is he? (*Pause*) Ah, there you are! (*The dragging steps resume*) That was a narrow squeak.

MR TYLER: I alit in the nick of time.

MRS ROONEY: It is suicide to be abroad. But what is it to be at home, Mr Tyler, what is it to be at home? A lingering dissolution. Now we are white with dust from head to foot. I beg your pardon?

MR TYLER: Nothing, Mrs Rooney, nothing, I was merely cursing under my breath, God and man, under my breath, and the wet Saturday afternoon of my conception. My back tyre has gone down again. I pumped it hard as iron before I set out. And now I am on the rim.

MRS ROONEY: Oh what a shame!

MR TYLER: Now if it were the front I should not so much mind. But the back. The back! The chain! The oil! The grease! The hub! The brakes! The gear! No! It is too much!

It is necessary to quote that passage at length for those not familiar with the works of Beckett. It crystallises the style—the preoccupation with means of transport (dragging feet, Connolly's van, the bicycle, and later on a horse and cart); the juxtaposition of the apparently mundane with the apparently metaphysical ('They removed everything, you know, the whole . . . er . . . bag of tricks. Now I am grandchildless.' 'Gracious how you wobble!'); the slow continuum (the dragging feet) which seems to be occurring in a vacuum, and yet which fatalistically recognises the only too-obvious ravages of time. That is Beckett's vision of the human condition (or part of it anyway). What most critics seem to miss is the deep-seated ironic humour contained in almost everything Beckett writes. This is surely summed up in Mr Tyler's (genuine) cry of anguish about the profound messiness of the back parts of his bicycle. It would be just too pedantic to assume that Beckett means us to assume that Tyler's bicycle here represents LIFE. Mr Tyler is only referring to his bicycle—or is he? And it is exactly in this ambiguity that Beckett's creative tension lives. (Is Godot God? Who knows?) To over-analyse his work is to pluck the petals from a flower, one by one, in the hope of discovering the quintessence of the flower. An impossible task.

Again, in one of Beckett's greatest novels—*Molloy*—the bicycle appears in all its ambiguity, at once transporting Molloy across the surface of the earth, and at the same time mocking his infirmity. To investigate the symbolism of the bicycle, again, is a futile and pointless task. It is there. It exists. It both helps and hinders Molloy.

'This is how I went about it. I fastened my crutches to the crossbar, one on either side, I propped the foot of my stiff leg (I forget which, now they're both stiff) on the projecting front axle, and I pedalled with the other. It was a chainless bicycle, with a free wheel, if such a bicycle exists. Dear bicycle, I shall not call you bike, you were green, like so many of your generation, I don't know why. It is a pleasure to meet it again. To describe it at length would be a pleasure.'

Again, this passage gives the reader some idea of the power of Beckett's writing. The casual, almost bland way that Molloy's crutches are mentioned strikingly reminds the reader of the mortality of man. (Crutches! Another form of transport.) And, indeed, Molloy is reduced to his crutches in the novel:

'In the end I found it, half buried in a soft bush. I threw aside my crutches and took it in my hands by the saddle and the handlebars, intending to wheel it a little, back and forth, before getting on and leaving for ever this accursed place. But I pushed and pulled in vain, the wheels would not turn. It was as though the brakes were jammed, and heaven knows they were not, for my bicycle had no brakes. And suddenly overcome by a great weariness, in spite of the dying day when I always felt most alive, I threw the bicycle back in the bush and lay down on the ground, on the grass, careless of the dew, I never feared the dew.'

Molloy continues on his crutches, but eventually even his legs give way, and the first part of the book, where we finally take leave of him, finishes with Molloy crawling on his belly, using his crutches like grapnels, plunging them in to the undergrowth to get a grip. And so he continues on his way, dragging himself forward with his wrists.

Whether the bicycle has had more effect on Irish writers than those of any other nationality is a very debatable point—the bicycle is still a valid means of transport in rural Ireland—but it is of more than nominal interest to note that another serious Irish writer has used the bicycle as an instrument of great comic invention. Flann O'Brien (who died in 1966) wrote a seminal novel in 1939, *At-Swim-Two-Birds* which is only now being recognised as a work of genius. Shortly after that (1940) he wrote a novel called *The Third Policeman*, which was published for the first time in 1967. Although not quite as good as the first novel, it is still astounding in its hellish funniness, or as one critic said about it, 'It is also the grimmest, though not the least funny, of these novels, set in a merry Irish hell where helpless laughter ends in a moan of despair.' The central character of *The Third Policeman* is a murderer who is dead throughout the story, and inhabits a sort of eternal hell which he has earned by his crime. Inspired by the mad savant, De Selby (who is brilliantly introduced into the novel by means of footnotes), the narrator (who is un-named), is intent on devoting his whole life to a study in depth of the works of De Selby. Hence the murder—for money to further this cause. The murder having been done, and the black box containing the money not having been found, the narrator makes for the police barracks to elicit the help of the local constabulary in finding it (naturally). And in the local police station he meets Sergeant Pluck and Policeman MacCruickeen, who must be two of the wildest creations in twentieth-century literature. For the two policemen see the whole of life and human existence in terms of bicycles! (Wild ideas are two-a-penny—to create the idea and also *sustain* it throughout the length of a modern novel says more for Flann O'Brien's talent than anything else could.) On the narrator's entry to the police station, he is met with the question from Sergeant Pluck: 'Is it about a bicycle?' Such is the motivation of the two policemen that they go to the extent of drawing up five rules of wisdom. Sergeant Pluck explains:

'There are five in all. Always ask any questions that are to be asked and never answer any. Turn everything you hear to your own advantage. Always carry a repair outfit. Take left turns as much as possible. Never apply your front brake first.'

The Sergeant explains, 'If you follow them, you will save your soul and you will never get a fall on a slippy road.' The whole of this book is permeated with dialogue such as this, which, of course, out of context, does not give the overall hilarious humour of the work. One can only give morsels which hint at the total flavour of the whole. Here is the Sergeant talking about the high saddle:

'"The high saddle," said the Sergeant, "was invented by a party called Peters (to be pedantic, this is obviously a reference to Pedersen, mentioned in a previous chapter) that spent his life in foreign parts riding on camels and other lofty animals—giraffes, elephants and birds that can run like hares and lay eggs the size of the bowl you see in a steam laundry where they keep the chemical water for taking the tar out of men's pants. When he came home from the wars he thought hard of sitting on a low saddle and one night accidentally when he was in bed he invented the high saddle as the outcome of his perpetual cerebration and mental researches . . . The high saddle was the father of the low handlebars, it crucifies the fork and gives you a blood rush in the head, it is very sore on the internal organs" "Which of the organs?", I enquired. "Both of them," said the Sergeant.'

To say that Flann O'Brien's sense of the absurd was acute would be to flaunt absurdity itself. About a third way through the novel, we come across a long passage, which, to call comic, would be to find oneself accused of being over-serious, or half-blind, or something. This is the passage in which the Sergeant reveals his reasons for stealing a particular person's bicycle every Monday, allowing him to find it every Tuesday. It is the passage in which Pluck expounds his explosively funny theory about the Atomic Theory. It runs something like this: If a man rides a bicycle, day by day, for a long enough period over the rocky roads of the parish, the atoms of the bicycle will, eventually, be transferred into the body of the rider, and the atoms of the rider will be transferred in to the body of the bicycle. To describe it in such bald terms is to shear it of the beautiful and hilarious dialogue in which Sergeant Pluck propounds it. There is only one word for it: Crazy Cartesian. Says Pluck: 'You would be surprised at the number of people in these parts who nearly are half people and half bicycles.'

Given that premise, O'Brien takes it to its mad logical conclusion. There are men riding girls' bicycles, and girls riding mens' bicycles, in the parish. 'Need I inform you what the result was or what happened?' ask the Sergeant, eyebrows dark and knowing.

Nor is that the end of the logicality. Pluck, to prove finally his theory to the unbeliever, evokes the memory of his great-grandfather. His great-grandfather, he claims, was, for a full year before his death, a horse, And, not only that, his old horse, Dan, was also in the contrary way. While the great-grandfather enjoyed himself jumping over hedges and galloping down the road, the horse, Dan, would come into the house at night and interfere with young girls. Eventually the police had the family shoot the horse, otherwise they would have to arrest him and have him up at the next Petty Sessions. But Pluck has other theories: 'If you ask me it was my great-grandfather they shot, and it is the horse that is buried up in Cloncoonla Churchyard.'

To continue quoting from Flann O'Brien's masterpiece would be to paraphrase, and that would be to dilute. Suffice to say that no other writer on earth has ever extracted such humour from the bicycle—and no one can do that unless they have a profound feeling for the magicality of the machine. Indeed, one could go so far as to say that *The Third Policeman* will go down in history, (for those interested in such things) as the definitive novel about the bicycle, and also, (for those also interested in such things) as one of the funniest books of this century. What better note to end a chapter on than Pluck's description of the village postman (who has been riding a bicycle all his life):

'If he walks too slowly or stops in the middle of the road he will fall down in a heap and will have to be lifted and set in motion again by some extraneous party. This is the unfortunate state that the postman has cycled himself into, and I do not think he will ever cycle himself out of it again.'

12

SADDLE-BAG OF ANECDOTES

'Great Britain isn't as advanced as we are. Probably half the people still ride bicycles.'

(From an essay by an American school-child 1967)

It is difficult to write the final chapter to a book on the bicycle. What is it to be: the red tail light, receding into the distance, winking mischievously and wobbling slightly from side to side; the messy rear part of the machine which evoked such a cry of anguish from Beckett's Mr Tyler; or the saddle bag, containing the hotch potch of spanners, oil rags, and bits of string of anecdotage, memories and things half-forgotten? One fights against it, but one knows it will be the saddle bag.

But not even the cyclist knows what the saddle bag contains —he, in fact, least of all. One could pull out the story of the cyclist who fitted a small motor to his machine, and, thereby, was legally enforced to take a driving test. Failing the first time, he was discreetly advised by the friendly driving examiner to turn up at his next test with the bicycle *minus* the engine. Gratefully, he did. He failed again.

Or one could tell of George Bernard Shaw, at the height of his fame, living in his cottage in Hertfordshire, in which he had installed a static bicycle (a home trainer), and to which he had recourse when inspiration failed him at the typewriter. (By all accounts he used to spend up to an hour on the infernal machine, after which time he would return to his work, suitably refreshed.) Or the other beautiful story about Shaw, when he invited Bertrand Russell to his place for the weekend. Russell, slightly bewildered at being told to alight from the train at a station which he knew was at least ten miles from Shaw's home, was surprised to be greeted by Shaw, on the station platform, armed with two bicycles. 'We will ride the ten miles,' Shaw is reported to have said, smilingly. 'We will not,' Russell is reported to have answered, the meantime enquiring of the station porter the time of the next train to Shaw's village. The next train came along, Russell boarded it, and, according to Russell's own account, Shaw cycled furiously from station to station (there being three stations in between), arriving at the same time as the train, tramping onto the platform, and shouting abuse at Russell through the window.

Or one could tell of the young woman who rode her bicycle frequently across the border between one European country and another. In fact she rode it across so frequently that the border guards become used to it and very friendly with her, albeit on a smile and nod basis. They merely waved her on with a smile. However, on one particular occasion, having waved her on, she had great difficulty in mounting the bicycle, so much so that the machine fell over. One of the border guards, a friendly type, ran to help her. He got quite a surprise, however, when he discovered that he could not lift the bicycle. Suspicions aroused, the young woman was detained and the bicycle thoroughly examined. The tubular steel sections of the bike were discovered to contain gold, which had been melted down and poured into the tubes for smuggling.

But that (this being a saddle-bag) is a far cry from the correspondence which was hotly initiated by an article by Mr Stephen Potter (of *Gamesmanship* fame) which was published in *The Observer* in 1957, and in which Mr Potter described the bicycle as a 'push-bike'. Immediately, Mr Derek Roberts, a founder member of the Southern Veteran-Cycle Club and also editor of that club's magazine, *The Boneshaker*, dashed into print: He wrote a letter to Stephen Potter:

'Dear Sir, I was pained to read in today's *Observer,* your reference to "push-bikes". In the past I have found that few users of that term know how offensive it sounds to those who actually cycle for pleasure, and I am sure that you will not mind my little protest. It is, of course, permissible to use the designation in a "lifemanship" ploy. Similarly, I have at times been known to say, "I gave up riding stink-bikes"—after I sold the fifth—"too much noise and dirt" or, "I'm going to cycle over to see the Old Crocks run". But these have been recognised gambits; and the second would never be used in conversation with someone who couldn't recognise a gambit when he heard one. For a slightly different reason I should never refer to the motor-cars at Beaulieu as "old crocks". Lord Montague (a member of this club) would be as pained as we are when we see that Mr Potter refers to bicycles and tricycles as "push-bikes". Perhaps the clearest explanation would be to say that "push-bike" is a term that would be used by G. Odoreida when he was not gambitting.
Yours faithfully,
Derek Roberts.'

Mr Stephen Potter replied:

'Dear Mr Roberts,
Your letter pained me. You surely must realise that to a vast area of Southern England "push-bike" is a term of familiarity of a kind reserved for institutions which have achieved absolute honourableness in public opinion, unshakeable affection in the public heart and a dignity so unassailable that the use of a comic nickname is in itself a comic admission of the absolute disparity between the

unworthiness of the nicknamer and the final goodness of the nickname. Compare "Winnie". Compare "ping pong" for my favourite game of table tennis.
Yours sincerely,
Stephen Potter.'

Mr Roberts answered:

'Dear Mr Potter,
Thank you for your charming little letter. I must confess that I do feel rather badly about things now. I had not realised that my mild reproof would make you so conscious of your shortcomings when compared with the bicycle; I do hope that you have not become the victim of some dreadful complex.
Yours sincerely,
Derek Roberts.'

Like most saddle-bags, this one produces violent contrasts. The following is from a newspaper of May, 1967:

'White is their colour, anarchy their banner, hypocrisy their enemy, collective fun their pursuit.'

Briefly, it is a description of the Dutch Provos, that band of young Dutch people who have rejected the conventionality of their fathers, anticipated the 'hippies' of the USA and the UK by a number of years and, above all, adopted the bicycle as their symbol—the White Bicycle. (This has also been, belatedly, adopted by the Hampstead Theatre Club of London as a symbol of live theatre—two white bicycles adorn the roof of the theatre.) One of the leading Dutch Provos is Luud Schimmelpenninck, a 30-year-old who has made his living so far out of inventing a plastic bicycle. Schimmelpenninck is not only an elected member of the Amsterdam City Council, but is also the architect of the White Bicycle Plan. According to the White Bicycle Plan, the City of Amsterdam should buy 20,000 bicycles, paint them white and turn them loose on the city to be used as public transport, to be abandoned in the street after use.

The centre of the city would be painted white and all motor-cars would be banned from that area. An impractical idea for London and New York, but perhaps not for Amsterdam?

Out of the rag-bag saddle-bag, perhaps the cyclist himself may be allowed to draw a personal belonging. A mythical bicycle. One such exists and was invented by the author of this book some years ago. It happened like this.

In 1964, Mr Iain Shaw was drama critic for the weekly newspaper *Tribune*. In that year, the Royal Court Theatre had revived Samuel Beckett's *Waiting for Godot*. Mr Shaw took the opportunity to attack not only the whole concept of the play as such, but the basis of Beckett's writing. The following week, the author of this book, in the columns of *Tribune* defended Beckett against Shaw's criticism, ending his defence by writing: 'Come off it, Mr Shaw. Beckett's bicycle is not Cartesian —it's bloody well rural Irish!'

The following week, a mutual friend of both Mr Shaw and the author, met the latter in a pub and the conversation went as follows:

FRIEND: Iain liked your defence of Beckett this week.
S. MCG: Good—glad to hear it.
FRIEND: Yes, he thought that between himself and yourself, if people read between the lines, they might get an idea of what Beckett was getting at.
S. MCG: Good, good.
Pause. Drink. Longer pause.
FRIEND: By the way . . . What *is* a Cartesian bicycle?
S. MCG: (*without a pause*) It is a fair machine, where the inner tube is the outer tube, the diamond frame is a ruby, the front wheel is at the back and the back wheel is God knows where, and when you think you're riding in a straight line you're riding in a circle . . .

BOOKS QUOTED

In writing this book, quotations have been made from the following works, and grateful acknowledgment is made to the authors and publishers:

If You See Me Comin', by Adrian Mitchell (Jonathan Cape, London).

All that Fall, by Samuel Beckett (Faber and Faber, London).

Molloy, by Samuel Beckett (Caldar and Boyars, London).

The Third Policeman, by Flann O'Brien (MacGibbon & Kee, London).

Me and My Bike, by Dylan Thomas (Triton, London).

Wheels of Chance, by H. G. Wells (J. M. Dent & Sons, Ltd., London).

Three Men on the Bummel, by Jerome K. Jerome (J. M. Dent & Sons Ltd., London).

BOOKS CONSULTED

The following works have also been consulted, and grateful acknowledgment is made to the authors and publishers:

The History and Development of Cycles, by C. F. Caunter (London, HMSO).

Early Bicycles, by Philip Sumner (Hugh Evelyn, London).

Riding High, by Arthur Judson Palmer (Vision Press, London).

Wheels Within Wheels, by Geoffrey Williamson (Geoffrey Bles, London).

Cycling is My Life, by Tommy Simpson (Stanley Paul, London).

The Tour de France, by Peter Clifford (Stanley Paul, London).

The Indo-China War, 1945-54, by Edgar O'Ballance (Faber and Faber, London).

INDEX

INDEX